# *Jo Verso*

# CROSS STITCH  CARDS & KEEPSAKES

*with charts and line illustrations*
*by the author*

**David & Charles**

*To Heather Moore, who dreamed up the idea*

*Hoping always for a meeting
With a friend I love so true,
Dear, I send this simple greeting,
May the world deal well with you.*

Verse from a Victorian greetings card

**British Library Cataloguing in Publication Data**
Verso, Jo
Cross stitch cards and keepsakes.
1. Embroidery, Cross-stitch
I. Title
746.443

Hardback ISBN 0-7153-9498-3
Paperback ISBN 0-7153-0374-0

First published 1990
First published in paperback 1996

© Jo Verso 1990

Typeset by Typesetters (Birmingham) Ltd
and printed in Italy
by LEGO SpA, Vicenza
for David & Charles
Brunel House  Newton Abbot  Devon

Distributed in the United States by
Sterling Publishing Co Inc
387 Park Avenue South, New York, NY 10016-8810

# Contents

| | | | |
|---|---|---|---|
| Introduction | 5 | Marriage | 64 |
| Calendar of Festivals | 6 | Wedding Anniversaries | 72 |
| Christmas | 8 | Babies | 76 |
| The Early Year | 24 | Christenings | 84 |
| Valentines | 32 | Religious Occasions | 87 |
| Easter | 36 | Festivals Worldwide | 92 |
| Mother's and Father's Days | 40 | Special Wishes | 100 |
| 4th July | 44 | The Final Curtain | 109 |
| Hallowe'en | 48 | Alphabets and Templates | 114 |
| Harvest and Thanksgiving | 50 | Techniques | 119 |
| Birthdays | 52 | Acknowledgements | 127 |
| Special Birthdays | 58 | Index | 128 |

# Introduction

Since the introduction of the penny post in Victorian times the sending of greetings cards has become an increasingly popular way of showing our affection and regard for others. Commercially produced cards are sent in their millions every year, most of which are thrown away soon after they are received, but cards which are hand-made for a special occasion are kept and treasured as keepsakes. They will be enjoyed for the personal thought and the skill which have gone into them, and their sentimental value will last a lifetime.

Cross stitch embroiderers who are hard pressed for time, or who might be daunted by a large piece of work, will appreciate that the designs in this book are on a small scale. Once the basic stitches have been mastered, most of the cards and keepsakes are quick and simple to produce with the minimum of materials. The effort involved should be more than repaid by the pleasure gained by those who receive them.

If you have read my first book, *Picture It in Cross Stitch*, you will see that this book provides more material to help you produce your own designs. You may be tempted to try adding your own touches to the designs, for example names, dates and other details. Do not hesitate to do so. The designs in both books are complementary and by using the material in both you can produce your own unique designs. For example, the photograph opposite shows how Design 52 has been expanded using other material in this book to produce a more personal result. So be adventurous; instructions on designing are included, and, if you doubt your own ability, what have you got to lose except a sheet of graph paper?

Be flexible in your approach to mounting the finished embroidery; many designs which have been made up as keepsakes can be turned into cards equally successfully. Similarly, many designs which appear as cards could be produced as keepsakes.

*To greet the birth of Princess Beatrice. Design 52 has been expanded using other material in the book to make a personalised keepsake*

Designs have been kept on a small scale to enable them to be mounted into greetings cards; this has been achieved by making use of three-quarter cross stitches and back stitch, in addition to full cross stitches. Before stitching a design, it is important for beginners to practise all stitches until they can produce them with ease. For traditionalists, some designs are included which contain no three-quarter cross stitches.

For each project, a photograph, a chart, a colour key and a list of materials needed to make it is provided. In order to avoid repetition, instructions on stitching and mounting which are common to many designs are placed at the end of the book.

Colour keys are provided to help you achieve a similar result to the samples in the photographs, but again, be adventurous, you do not have to follow the suggestions slavishly.

Thread numbers for both Anchor and DMC stranded cottons are given, but it must be stressed that the two ranges are not identical and therefore it is impossible to give an exact match when translating a thread number. Check your threads before you start to sew and make sure that you are happy with them, making any adjustments you feel are necessary. Do not attempt to match your threads to the colours of the charts; the colours available for the art work in the book are far less subtle than the wide range of threads available for embroidery.

The mounting of the finished embroidery has been kept as simple as possible to make it a less daunting task. If you follow the instructions, you should have no difficulty in achieving a result which looks hand-made rather than home-made. However, if the prospect of working with card, glue and a craft knife does not bring back happy memories of the time you spent at primary school, then let the wide range of ready-made card mounts which are now available come to your rescue. The presentation of a beautiful piece of hand embroidery can make or mar it, but do not be put off doing the embroidery because you lack the confidence to mount it; if all else fails you can always approach your friendly neighbourhood picture framer who will cut card mounts accurately for you.

# Calendar of Festivals

*1 January* . . . New Year's Day.

*25 January* . . . Burns' Night. Celebrated in Scotland to honour the poet Robert Burns who was born on 25 January 1759.

*21 January – 20 February* . . . Chinese New Year. The date changes annually according to the lunar calendar.

*26 January* . . . Australia Day. Commemorates the founding of the colony of New South Wales in 1788.

*2 February* . . . Candlemas. The Christian Feast of the Purification commemorating when the Child Jesus was brought to the Temple.

*3 February – 9 March* . . . Shrove Tuesday (Pancake Day or Mardi Gras) falls between these dates.

*6 February* . . . New Zealand Day, or Waitangi.

*14 February* . . . St Valentine's Day, the patron saint of lovers.

*Late February/early March* . . . Meelad ul-Nabi. Celebration of the birth of the Prophet Muhammad.

*Late February/early March* . . . Purim, a Jewish festival, a reminder of how the Jewish people living in Persia were saved from destruction.

*Late February/early March* . . . Holi. A Hindu festival which celebrates the end of winter and the beginning of spring.

*1 March* . . . St David's Day. The feast day of the patron saint of Wales.

*4 March – 7 April* . . . Mothering Sunday, a day on which mothers are honoured. Falls on the 4th Sunday in Lent.

*17 March* . . . St Patrick's Day. The feast day of the patron saint of Ireland.

*22 March – 24 April* . . . Easter. A Christian festival celebrating the resurrection of Jesus from the dead. Falls on the Sunday following the first full moon appearing on or after 21 March.

*27 March – 24 April* . . . The Jewish festival of Passover falls between these dates.

*1 April* . . . All Fool's Day.

*23 April* . . . St George's Day. Feast day of the patron saint of England.

*April* (date changes annually) . . . Baisakhi. Celebration of the Sikh New Year.

*1 May* . . . May Day, or Labour Day.

*Vesak* . . . The most important Buddhist festival which celebrates the life of the Buddha and takes place on, or near to, the May full moon.

*Ascension Thursday* . . . Christian festival which falls 40 days after Easter.

*Whitsuntide* . . . Christian festival which falls 10 days after Ascension Thursday.

*May – early June* . . . Sharuot. A Jewish festival which falls 50 days after Passover.

*June* . . . Father's Day. Falls on the 3rd Sunday in June.

*Midsummer* . . . Chinese Dragon Boat festival. Falls on the 5th day of the 5th month in the Chinese lunar calendar, somewhere near Midsummer's Day.

*1 July* . . . Dominion Day, Canada.

*4 July* . . . American Independence Day, USA.

*14 July* . . . Bastille Day, France.

*Ramadan* . . . the Muslim fast which moves through the different seasons of the year, but is always the 9th month of the Muslim lunar calendar.

*Id ul-Fitr* . . . Celebrated by Muslims at the end of Ramadan.

*Rosh Hashanah* . . . The Jewish New Year. Lasts for 10 days, usually in September or early October.

*Yom Kippur* . . . The Jewish Day of Atonement which follows the 10 days of Rosh Hashanah.

*September* . . . Harvest Festival or Harvest Home.

*October* . . . Diwali, the Hindu Festival of Lights. May fall in October or November.

*31 October* . . . Hallowe'en.

*1 November* . . . All Saints' Day.

*5 November* . . . Guy Fawkes' Night, or Bonfire Night.

*November* . . . Thanksgiving (USA). Falls on the 4th Thursday in November. (In Canada Thanksgiving is celebrated on the 2nd Monday in October.)

*30 November* . . . St Andrew's Day. Feast day of the patron saint of Scotland.

*6 December* . . . St Nicholas' Day in northern Europe.

*Chanukkah* . . . The Jewish Festival of Lights. Lasts 8 days and is held sometime in early December.

*25 December* . . . Christmas Day, the Christian celebration of the birth of Christ.

**FURTHER READING**
Purton, Rowland, *Festivals and Celebrations* (Blackwell, 1981).
Verso, Jo, *Picture It in Cross Stitch* (David & Charles, 1988).

# Christmas

# NATIVITY SCENE

Stitch on cream Zweigart 'Linda', 27 threads to 1in (2.5cm).
Finished size – 5×3¼in (12.7× 8.2cm).
Cut fabric to fit a 7in (18cm) embroidery hoop.

TO MOUNT
Follow the mounting instructions (Method 1) on p122.
*You will need:*
☐ 1 white Framecraft CraftaCard with a window 5½× 3¾in (14×9.5cm)

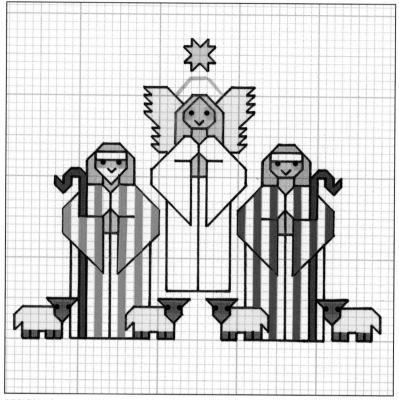

DESIGN 1A                    DESIGN 1B

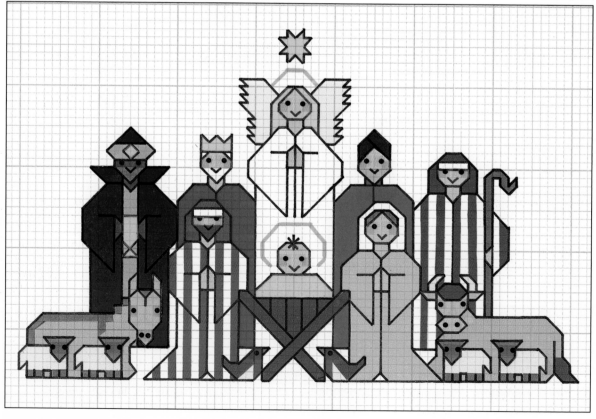

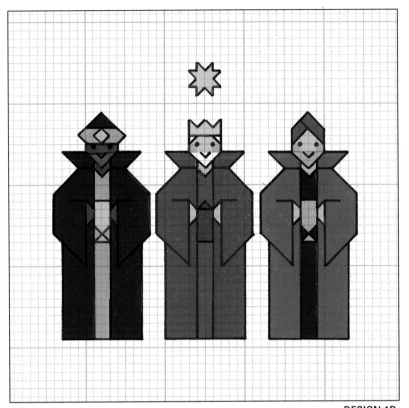

DESIGN 1C

DESIGN 1D

| DESIGN 1A, B, C, D | | |
|---|---|---|
| ANCHOR | | DMC |
| 0361 | ■ | 738 |
| 0175 | ■ | 794 |
| 0148 | ■ | 311 |
| 0185 | ■ | 964 |
| 0230 | ■ | 909 |
| 0301 | ■ | 744 |
| 0386 | □ | 746 |
| 01 | □ | blanc |
| 0349 | ■ | 301 |
| 0100 | ■ | 552 |
| 013 | ■ | 349 |
| 0400 | ■ | 645 |
| 0398 | ■ | 415 |
| 06 | ■ | 754 |
| 09 | ■ | 760 |
| **FRENCH KNOTS** | | |
| 0401 | ● | 844 |
| **BACK STITCH** | | |
| 0401 | – | 844 |
| 0301 | – | 744 |

The Nativity Scene has been used to produce other small cards. There are many other combinations of the material in the main design which could be used; for example, Jesus, Mary and Joseph could be placed with one shepherd and one king. If you are tempted to try your hand at designing your own unique cards using the design material here, consult the instructions on p119.
Mount the finished results in ready-made card mounts.

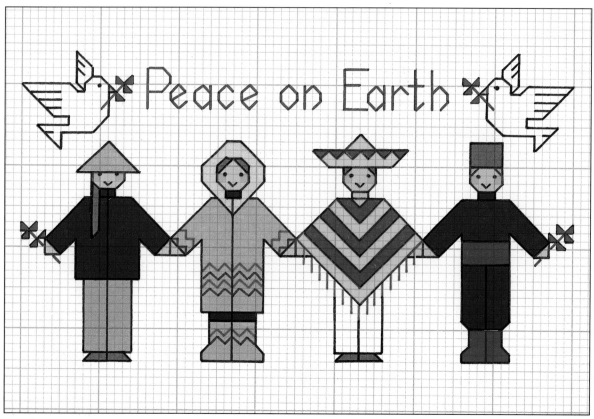

DESIGN 2

# PEACE ON EARTH

Stitch on cream deluxe Hardanger, Zweigart 'Oslo', 22 blocks to 1in (2.5cm).
Finished size – 6¼×3½in (15.9×8.9cm).
Cut fabric to fit an 8in (20cm) embroidery hoop.

TO MOUNT
Follow the mounting instructions (Method 2) on p123.
*You will need:*
☐ White card – 16×6in (40.6×15cm) to make a side-folded card
☐ White backing card – 8×6in (20.3×15cm)
☐ Window template – 63 squares × 45, cut from graph paper which has 10 squares to 1in (2.5cm)

| DESIGN 2 | | | | | |
|---|---|---|---|---|---|
| ANCHOR | | DMC | ANCHOR | | DMC |
| 01 | ☐ | blanc | 09 | ■ | 760 |
| 0301 | ■ | 444 | 0923 | ■ | 699 |
| 09046 | ■ | 321 | BACK STITCH | | |
| 0137 | ■ | 792 | 0403 | – | 310 |
| 0367 | ☐ | 422 | 0923 | – | 699 |
| 0386 | ☐ | 746 | 09046 | – | 321 |
| 0232 | ■ | 452 | 0137 | – | 792 |
| 0403 | ■ | 310 | FRENCH KNOTS | | |
| 06 | ■ | 754 | 0403 | ● | 310 |

12

DESIGN 3

# GOODWILL
# TO ALL MEN

Stitch on cream deluxe
Hardanger, Zweigart 'Oslo', 22
blocks to 1in (2.5cm).
Finished size – 5½×4in (14×
10.2cm).
Cut fabric to fit an 8in (20cm)
embroidery hoop.

TO MOUNT
Follow the mounting
instructions (Method 2) on
p123.
*You will need:*
☐ White card – 8×12in (20.3×
30cm) to make a top-folded card
☐ White backing card – 8×6in
(20.3×15cm)
☐ Window template – 60
squares × 44, cut from graph
paper which has 10 squares to
1in (2.5cm)

| DESIGN 3 | | | | | |
|---|---|---|---|---|---|
| ANCHOR | | DMC | ANCHOR | | DMC |
| 01 | ☐ | blanc | 0347 | ■ | 402 |
| 0403 | ■ | 310 | 0943 | ■ | 3045 |
| 0399 | ◻ | 318 | **BACK STITCH** | | |
| 0367 | ◻ | 422 | 0403 | – | 310 |
| 09046 | ■ | 321 | 0923 | – | 699 |
| 0133 | ■ | 796 | 09046 | – | 321 |
| 0109 | ◻ | 209 | **FRENCH KNOTS** | | |
| 0923 | ■ | 699 | 0403 | ● | 310 |
| 06 | ◻ | 754 | 09046 | ● | 321 |
| 0944 | ■ | 869 | | | |

# ADVENT CALENDAR

The effort of making this Advent Calendar for a child is repaid every year as you watch them discovering a tiny gift each day during the countdown to Christmas.

Stitch on cream deluxe Hardanger, Zweigart 'Oslo', 22 blocks to 1in (2.5cm).
Finished size – 11½×14½in (29.2×36.8cm).
Cut fabric 20×22in (51×56cm).
Add the name of the child at the top, using the alphabet (Fig 15) on p116 and the design instructions on p119. Adjust the number of berries and leaves to fit the remaining space. When the embroidery is complete, sew on 24 × 19mm brass curtain rings, one for each day, at the position marked on the chart.

TO MOUNT
*You will need:*
☐ Hardboard – 14×16in (36×41cm)
☐ Cotton fabric to cover the hardboard
☐ Cord for lacing

The hardboard needs to be covered with cotton fabric to ensure that there is no contact between it and the embroidery. Take care to choose a fabric that is plain and of a colour which will not show through. An old, white cotton pillowcase is ideal. Using a strong button thread or fine cord, lace the work in place on the back of the board from side to side and from top to bottom (Fig 1), checking that the lines on the front of the calendar are straight. A good framer will undertake the task for you if you prefer.

TO TRIM
*You will need:*
☐ 24 matchboxes – 37×53mm
☐ Christmas wrapping paper
☐ Adhesive
☐ 24 paper fasteners
☐ 5½yd (5m) Offray Red (250) 1.5mm ribbon
☐ 24 sweets or small gifts

To prepare a matchbox to hang on the Advent Calendar, cut a piece of wrapping paper to cover the sleeve section of the matchbox and glue the wrapping paper around the box sleeve. Pierce a hole centrally in the end of the drawer section of the matchbox, using a needle or other sharp instrument. Pass the prongs of a paper fastener through the hole and open them out on the inside (Fig 2). This provides a knob on the outside of the

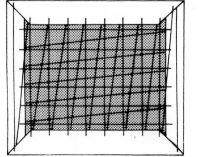 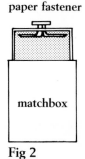

paper fastener

matchbox

**Fig 2**

**Fig 1** *Lacing work onto hardboard*

drawer onto which you can attach the ribbon. Cut the ribbon into 24 × 8in (20cm) lengths and tie a length around each paper fastener knob. Fill the prepared matchboxes with sweets or gifts and finally tie each one to the curtain rings.
Designs 1, 3, 6, 9, 10, 14, 19 and 23 of the Advent Calendar, stitched on Zweigart 'Linda', have been mounted in 2½in (6.3cm) round frames from Framecraft to make tree decorations. Designs 11, 13, 20, 21 and 23, if stitched on Zweigart 'Linda', will fit Framecraft 1½in (3.8cm) round mini frames, or can be mounted as gift tags using ready-made mounts available from Impress. Any of the designs can be stitched singly to make small cards which fit easily into a selection of ready-made card mounts.

| DESIGN 4A, B, C, D | | | | | |
|---|---|---|---|---|---|
| ANCHOR | | DMC | ANCHOR | | DMC |
| 09046 | ■ | 321 | 0231 | ■ | 453 |
| 0230 | ■ | 909 | 06 | ■ | 754 |
| 0204 | ■ | 954 | 09 | ■ | 760 |
| 0132 | ■ | 797 | **BACK STITCH** | | |
| 0144 | ■ | 3325 | 0403 | – | 310 |
| 0291 | ■ | 444 | 09046 | – | 321 |
| 01 | ☐ | blanc | 0230 | – | 909 |
| 0101 | ■ | 550 | 0291 | – | 444 |
| 0352 | ■ | 300 | **FRENCH KNOTS** | | |
| 0890 | ■ | 729 | 0403 | ● | 310 |
| 0925 | ■ | 970 | 09046 | ● | 321 |
| 0403 | ■ | 310 | | | |

**DESIGN 4A**

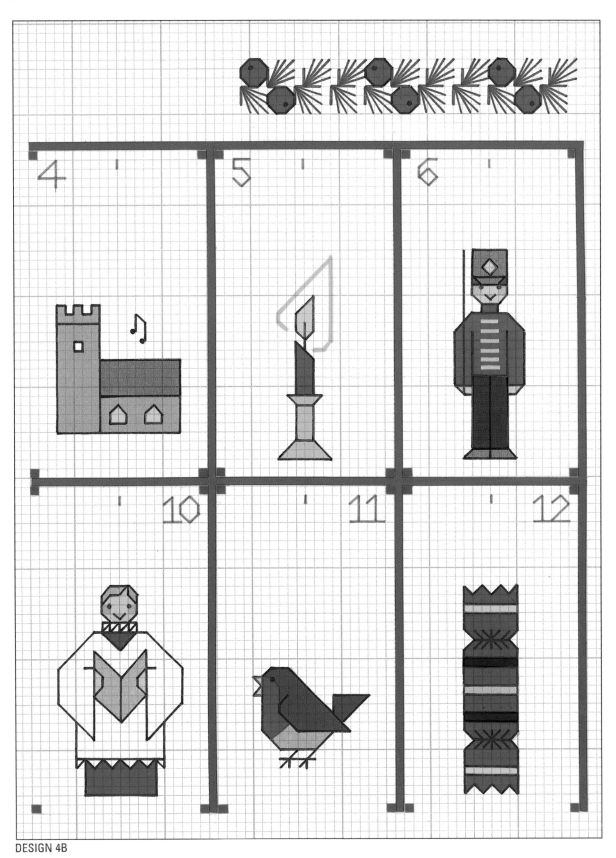

DESIGN 4B

DESIGN 4C

DESIGN 4D

# THE TWELVE DAYS OF CHRISTMAS

*'On the twelfth day of Christmas my true love sent to me:*
*Twelve lords a-leaping, eleven ladies dancing, ten drummers drumming, nine pipers piping,*
*eight maids a-milking, seven swans a-swimming,*
*six geese a-laying, five gold rings,*
*four calling birds, three French hens, two turtle doves and a partridge in a pear tree.'*

The traditional song has inspired a design for two bell-pulls to hang either side of the fire-place at Christmas time. Those with a really true love could use the designs to make twelve separate cards to send over the twelve days of Christmas. However, if you are not quite so devoted as this but have stamina, you might consider sending the set over a twelve-year period. The two turtle doves would make a suitable card for Valentine's Day, an engagement, wedding, or wedding anniversary.

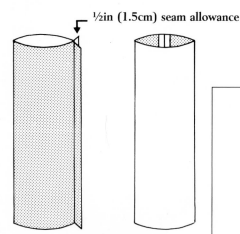

½in (1.5cm) seam allowance

**Fig 3** *Seaming and folding a hanging*

Stitch on cream deluxe Hardanger, Zweigart 'Oslo', 22 blocks to 1in (2.5cm).
Finished size – 19×3¼in (48×8.2cm).
Cut 2 pieces of fabric 9×24in (23×61cm).

TO MAKE UP
*You will need:*
☐ 2 pairs × 4in (10cm) brass bell-pull hangers
☐ White sewing thread

Fold the embroidery in half lengthwise, with right sides together. Allowing ½in (1.5cm) seam allowance, seam the two edges together to form a long tube. Turn right side out and press the fabric gently with a warm iron, avoiding the embroidery, so that the seam lies centrally at the back (Fig 3). Neaten the ends by turning them to the inside of the tube, top and bottom. Pass the ends through the hangers, fold to the back and stitch in place.

TO TRIM
*You will need:*
☐ 1yd (1m) each of 1in (25mm) red ribbon and 1in (25mm) tartan ribbon

Cut each ribbon into two equal lengths. Using a piece of red ribbon with a piece of tartan ribbon, make two bows. Trim the ends and sew a bow to the top of each bell pull.

| DESIGN 5A, B | | | | | |
|---|---|---|---|---|---|
| ANCHOR | | DMC | ANCHOR | | DMC |
| 01 | ☐ | blanc | 09 | ▨ | 760 |
| 09046 | ■ | 321 | 0900 | ▨ | 648 |
| 0230 | ■ | 909 | 0403 | ▨ | 310 |
| 0133 | ■ | 796 | BACK STITCH | | |
| 0160 | ▨ | 813 | 0403 | — | 310 |
| 0297 | ▨ | 726 | 0879 | — | 500 |
| 0304 | ▨ | 740 | 0297 | — | 726 |
| 0357 | ■ | 975 | FRENCH KNOTS | | |
| 0309 | ■ | 976 | 0403 | ● | 310 |
| 06 | ▨ | 754 | 09046 | ● | 321 |

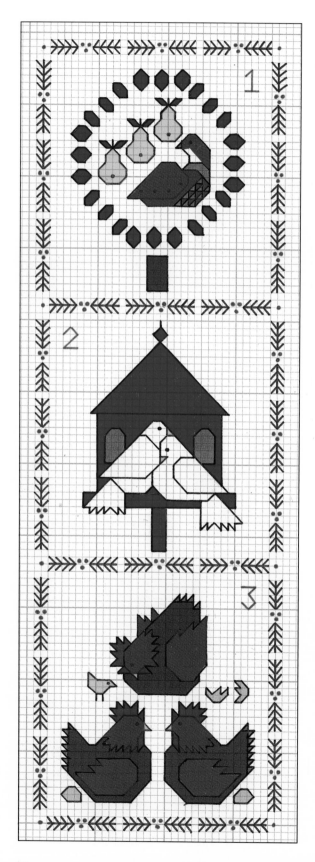

**DESIGN 5A**

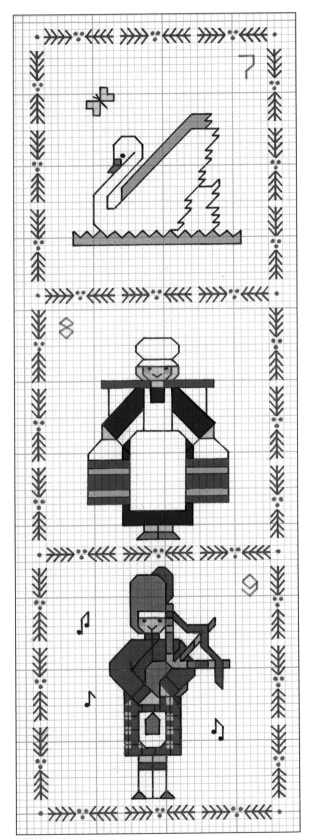

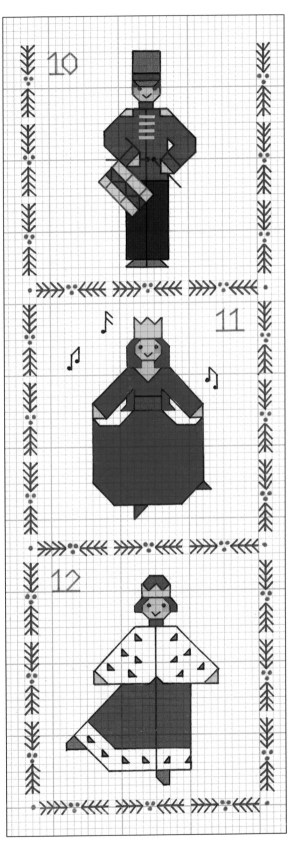

**DESIGN 5B**

# The Early Year

Calendar

Happy
Saint
Patrick's
Day

# NEW YEAR'S CALENDAR

Stitch on cream deluxe Hardanger, Zweigart 'Oslo', 22 blocks to 1in (2.5cm). Finished size – 6½×6¾in (16.5×17.1cm). Cut fabric to fit a 10in (25cm) embroidery hoop.

To work the border you will need 42in (106cm) each of Offray Willow (563) 3mm ribbon and Offray Forest Green (587) 3mm ribbon. Cut each length into two and use the lighter colour for the inner line. Couch the ribbons to the surface of the fabric (Fig 4) using large cross stitches as indicated on the chart. Tie the ends of the ribbons together into bows centrally at the top and the bottom and trim the ends.

TO MOUNT
Follow the mounting

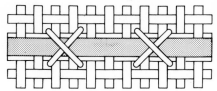

**Fig 4** *Couching ribbon onto fabric*

DESIGN 6

instructions (Method 2) on p123, cutting only sections a and b (Fig 40) and omitting the instructions to score and fold.
*You will need:*
☐ Pale green card – 8½×8½in (21.6×21.6cm)
☐ White backing card – 8½× 8½in (21.6×21.6cm)
☐ Window template – 70 squares × 70, cut from graph paper which has 10 squares to 1in (2.5cm)

When mounted, add a calendar tab centrally at the bottom, and a small hanging tab centrally on the back.

## DESIGN 6

| ANCHOR | | DMC |
|---|---|---|
| 0261 | ☐ | 966 |
| 0229 | ■ | 701 |
| 01 | ☐ | blanc |
| 0297 | ☐ | 726 |
| 0303 | ■ | 741 |
| 047 | ■ | 304 |
| 0975 | ☐ | 775 |

| ANCHOR | | DMC |
|---|---|---|
| 0143 | ■ | 797 |
| 0357 | ■ | 975 |
| 0401 | ■ | 844 |
| 06 | ☐ | 754 |
| 09 | ■ | 760 |

**BACK STITCH**

| ANCHOR | | DMC |
|---|---|---|
| 0403 | – | 310 |
| 047 | – | 304 |

| ANCHOR | | DMC |
|---|---|---|

**FRENCH KNOTS**

| ANCHOR | | DMC |
|---|---|---|
| 0403 | ● | 310 |
| 0229 | ● | 701 |
| 0297 | ● | 726 |
| 01 | ◘ | blanc |

**COUCHING STITCHES**

| ANCHOR | | DMC |
|---|---|---|
| 0229 | × | 701 |

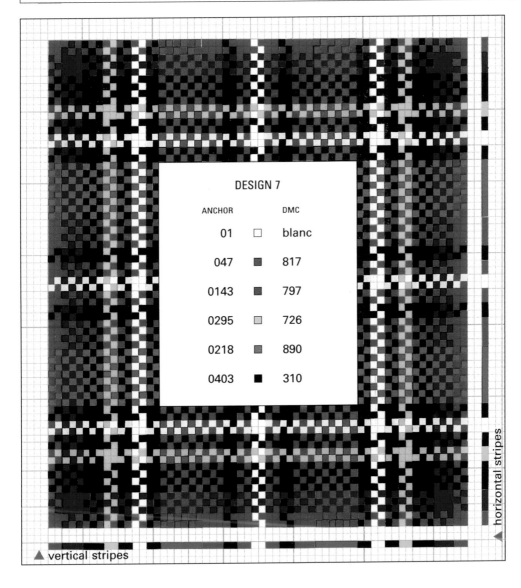

## DESIGN 7

| ANCHOR | | DMC |
|---|---|---|
| 01 | ☐ | blanc |
| 047 | ■ | 817 |
| 0143 | ■ | 797 |
| 0295 | ☐ | 726 |
| 0218 | ■ | 890 |
| 0403 | ■ | 310 |

▲ horizontal stripes

▲ vertical stripes

DESIGN 7
HOGMANAY (p28)

# HOGMANAY

Stitch on cream 'Aida', 18 blocks to 1in (2.5cm).
Finished size – 3½×3¾in (8.9× 9.5cm).
Cut fabric to fit a 6in (15cm) hoop.
At first glance this chart looks very daunting to work, but it is in fact simple if you use the bar codes printed at the bottom and the side of the chart. Starting at the bottom right-hand corner, work the first vertical red line (marked red in the bar code). You will see that it consists of working every other stitch in red to the top of the chart. The next line is red again so work down, embroidering every alternate stitch in red. Continue working across in this way following the colours on the bar code, working alternate stitches, until all the vertical stripes are complete. It is then a simple matter to fill in the horizontal stripes in the remaining spaces, again using the bar code as a guide. Add the date, using the alphabet (Fig 17) on p116 and the design instructions on p119.

TO MOUNT
Follow the mounting instructions (Method 2) p123.
*You will need:*
☐ Cream card – 5½×11in (14× 28cm) to make a top-folded card
☐ Cream backing card – 5½× 5½in (14×14cm)
☐ Window template – 35 squares × 39, cut from graph paper which has 10 squares to 1in (2.5cm)
Punch two holes in the side of the card and trim with a small bow of red ribbon.
To make the photograph frame, the design was stitched on 'Aida', 11 blocks to 1in (2.5cm), and was taken to a professional framer to have the embroidery mounted and framed.

DESIGN 8

# SAINT PATRICK'S DAY

A design based on Celtic knotwork.

Stitch on cream deluxe Hardanger, Zweigart 'Oslo', 22 blocks to 1in (2.5cm).
Finished size – 4×5¼in (10.2× 13.3cm).
Cut fabric to fit an 8in (20cm) embroidery hoop.

TO MOUNT
Follow the mounting instructions (Method 2) on p123.
*You will need:*
☐ White card – 8×12in (20.3× 30cm) to make a side-folded card
☐ White backing card – 8×6in (20.3×15cm)
☐ Window template – 40 squares × 53, cut from graph paper which has 10 squares to 1in (2.5cm)

This design can be used to make an attractive photograph frame if mounted in the same way as the Hogmanay frame on p25.

| DESIGN 8 | | |
|---|---|---|
| ANCHOR | | DMC |
| 0403 | ■ | 310 |
| 0143 | ■ | 797 |
| 0923 | ■ | 699 |
| 0291 | ■ | 444 |
| 09046 | ■ | 321 |
| **BACK STITCH** | | |
| 0403 | – | 310 |
| 0923 | – | 699 |
| **FRENCH KNOTS** | | |
| 0923 | ● | 699 |

# PATRON SAINT'S DAY BROOCHES

Make one of these and you will never be without your national emblem on the appointed day.

SAINT DAVID'S DAY
Designs 9 and 10
SAINT PATRICK'S DAY
Design 11
SAINT GEORGE'S DAY
Design 12
SAINT ANDREW'S DAY
Design 13

All the designs are stitched on cream Zweigart 'Belfast', 30 threads to 1in (2.5cm).
Cut fabric to fit a 4in (10cm) embroidery hoop.
Mount into 1in (2.5cm) circular or 1½in (3.8cm) oval Framecraft brooch mounts, following the manufacturer's instructions.

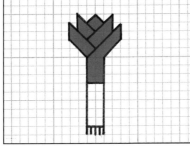

DESIGN 9

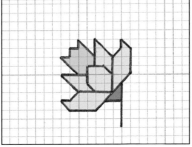

DESIGN 10

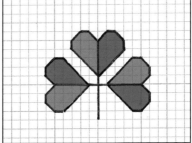

DESIGN 11

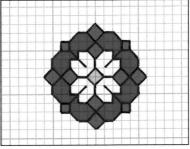

DESIGN 12

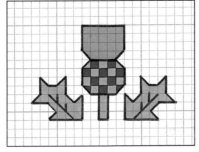

DESIGN 13

| DESIGN 9 | | |
|---|---|---|
| ANCHOR | | DMC |
| 0246 | ■ | 986 |
| 01 | □ | blanc |
| **BACK STITCH** | | |
| 0403 | – | 310 |
| **DESIGN 10** | | |
| 0295 | ■ | 726 |
| 0306 | ■ | 783 |
| 0243 | ■ | 989 |
| **BACK STITCH** | | |
| 0862 | – | 520 |
| **DESIGN 11** | | |
| 0246 | ■ | 986 |
| 0243 | ■ | 989 |
| **BACK STITCH** | | |
| 0246 | – | 986 |
| **DESIGN 12** | | |
| 059 | ■ | 326 |
| 01 | □ | blanc |
| 0874 | ■ | 834 |
| 0876 | ■ | 502 |
| **BACK STITCH** | | |
| 0401 | – | 844 |
| **DESIGN 13** | | |
| 0108 | ■ | 210 |
| 0879 | ■ | 500 |
| 0876 | ■ | 502 |
| **BACK STITCH** | | |
| 0879 | – | 500 |

# ALL FOOLS' DAY

Cryptic advice to the foolish makes up this conversation piece. The answer to the puzzle appears on p128.

Stitch on cream deluxe Hardanger, Zweigart 'Oslo', 22 blocks to 1in (2.5cm).
Finished size – 10¼×8¼in (26×21cm).
Cut fabric 16×14in (41×36cm).
If this design is stitched on a fine fabric, such as Zweigart 'Belfast', it will be small enough to mount as a card. This version was taken to a professional framer where it was mounted in an old text frame.

DESIGN 14A

| DESIGN 14A, B | | |
|---|---|---|
| ANCHOR | | DMC |
| 0876 | ■ | 502 |
| 0109 | ▨ | 210 |
| 066 | ▨ | 3688 |
| 0292 | ☐ | 3078 |
| 0874 | ▨ | 834 |
| 0926 | ☐ | écru |
| BACK STITCH | | |
| 0401 | – | 844 |
| FRENCH KNOTS | | |
| 0401 | ● | 844 |
| 0292 | ○ | 3078 |

DESIGN 14B

# Valentines

Roses are red
Violets blue
Honey is sweet
And so are you.

BE MINE

I LOVE YOU

# ROSES ARE RED

A drawstring bag to fill with a jar of honey or other love tokens.

Stitch on cream Zweigart 'Linda', 27 threads to 1in (2.5cm).
Finished size – 4½×3½in (11.4×8.9cm).
Cut fabric 6½×20in (16.5×52cm).
Fold the fabric in half, 6½×10in (16.5×26cm) and embroider the design centrally so that the bottom of the design lies 1in (2.5cm) up from the fold.

## TO MAKE UP
Follow the instructions for making a drawstring bag given on p124.

## TO TRIM
*You will need:*
☐ ½yd (50cm) narrow lace trimming
☐ 1½yd (1.5m) Offray Capri Blue (337) 3mm ribbon
☐ 3 violet flower beads, 2 leaf beads, 3 tiny yellow beads (optional)
Sew a strip of lace trimming to the top and bottom of the bag. Trim the drawstrings with flower and leaf beads.

| DESIGN 15 | | | | | | |
|---|---|---|---|---|---|---|
| ANCHOR | | DMC | | ANCHOR | | DMC |
| 0215 | ■ | 320 | | 0360 | ■ | 898 |
| 0118 | ■ | 340 | | 0386 | ☐ | 746 |
| 044 | ■ | 814 | | **BACK STITCH** | | |
| 059 | ■ | 326 | | 0403 | – | 310 |
| 040 | ■ | 899 | | 0215 | – | 320 |
| 0887 | ☐ | 3046 | | **FRENCH KNOTS** | | |
| | | | | 0403 | ● | 310 |

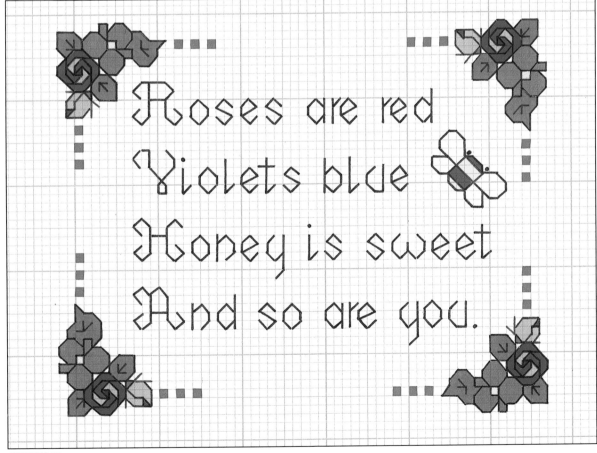

DESIGN 15

# VICTORIAN PIN PILLOW

A romantic offering stitched on red 'Aida', 18 blocks to 1in (2.5cm).
Finished size – 5½×6in (14× 15cm).
Cut fabric to fit an 8in (20cm) embroidery hoop.

On graph paper draw the left-hand side of the pattern, making it a mirror image of the right-hand side.

TO MAKE UP
*You will need:*
☐ Backing fabric of the same size as the 'Aida'
☐ Fibrefill stuffing
☐ 5ft (1.5m) of 1in (2.5cm) lace edging
☐ 1yd (1m) white narrow lace braid
☐ ¼yd (25cm) white daisy lace braid
☐ 1 packet each of rustless bridal pins, small red sequins, tiny red beads and tiny white beads
☐ 1 dusty pink ribbon rose
☐ ½yd (50cm) white 3mm ribbon, made into a multi-looped bow (Fig 46)

Pin the backing fabric to the 'Aida', right sides together and stitch the two together in a heart shape, ½in (1.5cm) from the edge of the embroidery, leaving a small opening for stuffing. Trim away the excess fabric and clip all curves. Turn right side out and stuff firmly with Fibrefill. Slipstitch the opening closed. Gather the lace edging to fit around the seam of the heart, and, distributing the gathers evenly, slipstitch in place. Cut lengths of lace braid; thread the pins with beads and use the beaded pins to anchor the braids in the positions shown on the

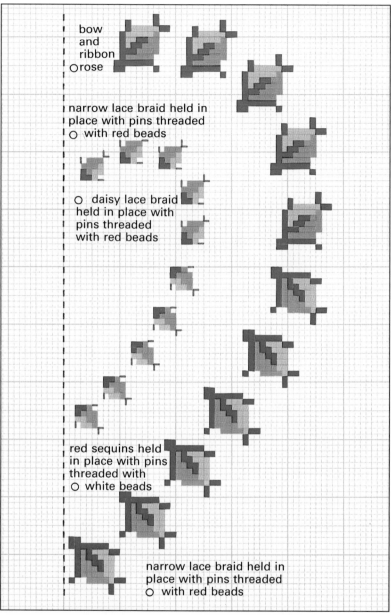

bow and ribbon ○ rose

narrow lace braid held in place with pins threaded ○ with red beads

○ daisy lace braid held in place with pins threaded with red beads

red sequins held in place with pins threaded with ○ white beads

narrow lace braid held in place with pins threaded ○ with red beads

chart. Pin the sequins to the pillow (Fig 34b) at regular intervals in the positions shown on the chart. Add a multi-looped bow and a ribbon rose at the top, between the rosebuds. Lastly spell out your message in pins in the central space.
For the cream heart, use cream 'Aida' and trim with cream laces, pearly white sequins, green and pink beads, a pale pink ribbon rose and a bow made from deep pink ribbon.

| DESIGN 16 | | |
|---|---|---|
| ANCHOR | | DMC |
| (0215) 0215 | ■ | 320 (320) |
| (077) 076 | ■ | 899 (335) |
| (075) 073 | ■ | 818 (3326) |
| BACK STITCH | | |
| (0215) 0215 | — | 320 (320) |

Colours for the cream pillow are given in brackets

# CUPID'S ARROW

Stitch on white Zweigart 'Linda', 27 threads to 1in (2.5cm).
Finished size – 3¾×3¼in (9.5× 8.2cm).
Cut fabric to fit a 6in (15cm) embroidery hoop.

## TO MOUNT
Follow the mounting instructions (Method 2) on p123.
*You will need:*
☐ White card – 5½×10½in (14×26.8cm) to make a top-folded card
☐ White backing card – 5½× 5¼in (14×13.4cm)
☐ Window template – 42 squares × 36, cut from graph paper which has 10 squares to 1in (2.5cm)

## TO TRIM
*You will need:*
☐ 1yd (1m) Offray Antique Blue (338) 1.5mm ribbon
☐ 1yd (1m) Offray Light Pink (117) 1.5mm ribbon
☐ 2 red heart beads (optional)

Thread the beads, if used, onto the ends of the pink ribbon (Fig 47). Tie the blue and pink ribbon in a bow around the fold of the card and trim to length. Sit back and wait for the arrow to find its mark.

| DESIGN 17 | | | | | |
|---|---|---|---|---|---|
| ANCHOR | | DMC | ANCHOR | | DMC |
| 0231 | ☐ | 453 | 0874 | ☐ | 3046 |
| 0920 | ☐ | 932 | 01 | ☐ | blanc |
| 0922 | ☐ | 930 | BACK STITCH | | |
| 06 | ☐ | 754 | 0400 | – | 317 |
| 09 | ☐ | 760 | FRENCH KNOTS | | |
| 011 | ☐ | 3328 | 0400 | ● | 317 |
| 0875 | ☐ | 503 | | | |

DESIGN 17

# Easter

He
is
risen

HAPPY
EASTER

HAPPY EASTER

| DESIGN 18 | | |
|---|---|---|
| ANCHOR | | DMC |
| 0204 | ■ | 913 |
| 0295 | □ | 726 |
| 0302 | ■ | 742 |
| 0109 | ■ | 209 |
| BACK STITCH | | |
| 0102 | – | 550 |
| (Writing, violets, outline of cross) | | |
| BACK STITCH | | |
| 0862 | – | 520 |
| (Daffodils, violet leaves) | | |
| FRENCH KNOTS | | |
| 0102 | ● | 550 |

DESIGN 18

# HE IS RISEN

Stitch on white Zweigart 'Linda', 27 threads to
1in (2.5cm).
Finished size – 3½×3½in (8.9×8.9cm).
Cut fabric to fit a 5in (13cm) embroidery hoop.

TO MOUNT
Follow the mounting instructions (Method 2) on
p123.
*You will need:*
☐ White card – 11×6½in (28×16.5cm) to make
a side-folded card
Cut a 4¼in (10.8cm) diameter circular window
in this card, using a compass cutter.
☐ White backing card – 5½×6½in (14×16.5cm)

TO TRIM
☐ 1yd (1m) Offray Mulberry (475) 3mm ribbon

Tie the ribbon in a bow around the fold and trim
to length.

# EASTER BONNET PINCUSHION

Stitch on cream Zweigart 'Linda', 27 threads to
1in (2.5cm).
Finished size – 2½in (6.3cm) diameter circle.
Cut fabric to fit a 6in (15cm) embroidery hoop.

TO MAKE UP
*You will need:*
☐ 1–2½in (6.3cm) diameter styrofoam ball, sawn
in half
☐ 1–4½in (11.5cm) diameter crochet doily
☐ 2×3¾in (9.5cm) diameter circles cut from thin
card
☐ 2×5in (12.7cm) diameter circles cut from fine
cream cotton fabric
☐ UHU glue

To make the crown, trim the embroidered fabric
to a 5½in (14cm) diameter circle. Sew a running
thread ½in (1.5cm) from the edge and pin the

| DESIGN 19 | | |
|---|---|---|
| ANCHOR | | DMC |
| 0109 | ◻ | 209 |
| 0131 | ◼ | 798 |
| 066 | ◻ | 3688 |
| 0301 | ◻ | 744 |
| 0215 | ◻ | 320 |
| 01 | ◻ | blanc |
| FRENCH KNOTS | | |
| 0301 | · | 744 |
| BACK STITCH | | |
| 0102 | — | 550 |
| 068 | — | 3687 |

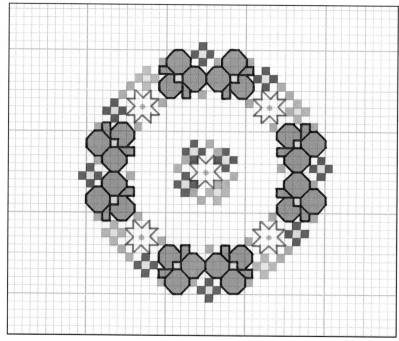

DESIGN 19

fabric in position on the ball. Pull up the running thread and, distributing all gathers evenly, tuck the raw edges of the fabric underneath the ball. Hold in place with a few pins. To make the brim, cover the card circles with the cotton fabric. Clip excess fabric and turn under, glueing in place. Glue the two circles together, wrong sides together. Glue the doily to the brim and finally glue the crown to the brim.

## TO TRIM
*You will need:*
☐ ½yd (50cm) white picot-edged 7mm ribbon
☐ ½yd (50cm) Offray Thistle (435) 3mm ribbon
☐ Small artificial flowers and white feathers

Tie a length of white ribbon around the brim. Add a length of mauve ribbon on top of the white. Glue on a mauve multi-looped bow (Fig 46), into which are tucked flowers and feathers. Lastly, add some rustless pins.

# EASTER GIFT TAG

Stitch on cream Zweigart 'Linda', 27 threads to 1in (2.5cm).
Finished size – 3×1in (7.6× 2.5cm).
Cut fabric to fit a 4in (10cm) embroidery hoop.
You can add a greeting using the alphabet (Fig 18) on p116 and the design instructions on p119. When the embroidery is complete attach a small, fluffy yellow feather to each egg.

## TO MOUNT
*You will need:*
☐ 2 pieces of white card cut from Template 1 on p118
☐ Double-sided sticky tape
☐ UHU glue
☐ ½yd (50cm) Offray Rosy Mauve (165) 1.5mm ribbon

Attach the embroidery to one of the pieces of card using double-sided sticky tape. Turn all raw edges to the back of the card and glue them down with UHU. Stick the other piece of card on the back of the tag. Sew the mauve ribbon to the tag, which can then be attached to an Easter gift.

DESIGN 20

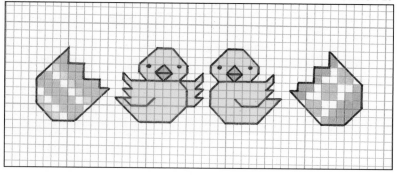

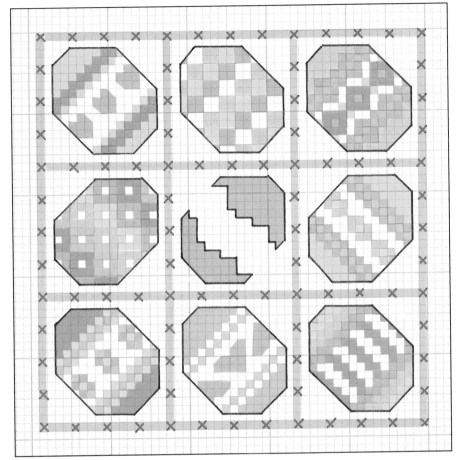

## DESIGN 20, 21

| ANCHOR | | DMC |
|--------|---|-----|
| 0302 | ◻ | 742 (Gift tag only) |
| 0204 | ◻ | 913 |
| 0301 | ◻ | 744 |
| 0111 | ◻ | 208 |
| 0130 | ◻ | 799 |
| 066 | ◻ | 3688 |
| 01 | ◻ | blanc |
| **BACK STITCH** | | |
| 0400 | – | 413 |
| **COUCHING STITCHES** | | |
| 0204 | ◻ | 913 |

DESIGN 21

# EASTER EGGS

Stitch on cream Zweigart 'Linda', 27 threads to 1in (2.5cm).
Finished size – 3½×3½in (9×9cm).
Cut fabric to fit a 6in (15cm) embroidery hoop.
To work the green dividing lines you will need 1yd (1m) of Offray Mint (530) 1.5mm ribbon cut into 8×4in (10.2cm) lengths. Couch down the ribbons with cross stitches (Fig 4) at the positions marked on the chart and cover the raw ends with the card mount. Alternatively, you can omit the ribbons and replace them with solid lines of cross stitches. When the embroidery is complete, glue a fluffy yellow feather to the 'hatched' egg in the centre of the design.

TO MOUNT
Follow the mounting instructions (Method 2) on p123.
*You will need:*
☐ Yellow card – 12×6½in (30.4×16.5cm) to make a side-folded card
☐ White backing card – 6×6½in (15.2×16.5cm)
☐ Window template – 36 squares × 36, cut from graph paper which has 10 squares to 1in (2.5cm)

TO TRIM
*You will need:*
☐ 1yd (1m) each of Offray Mint (530), Lemon (640), Rosy Mauve (165) and Antique Blue (338) 1.5mm ribbon

Tie the ribbons in a knot around the fold so that the loose ends cascade down the side of the card.

# Mother's and Father's Days

# POT-POURRI HEART SACHET

This small sachet is backed with net veiling which allows the fragrance to escape easily.

Stitch on cream Zweigart 'Linda', 27 threads to 1in (2.5cm).
Finished size – 3¼×2½in (8.2× 6.3cm).
Cut fabric to fit a 4in (10cm) embroidery hoop.

## TO MAKE UP
*You will need:*
□ A piece of net veiling – 5×4in (12.7×10.2cm)
□ 24in (61cm) × ¾in (2cm) lace
□ White sewing cotton
□ Pot-pourri
□ 12in (31cm) narrow lace braid
□ A small cream ribbon bow
□ 24in (61cm) each of Offray Red (250), Mulberry (475), Rosewood (169), Forest Green (587) and Wine (275) 3mm ribbon

Trace Template 2 on p118 onto the net veiling to give a seam line. Place the veiling over the embroidery, right sides together so that the seam line frames the flowers evenly. Sew around the seam line, leaving a small opening. Trim away the excess fabric ½in (1.5cm) from the line of stitching, clip all curves and

**DESIGN 22**

turn the sachet the right way out. Fill with pot-pourri and slipstitch closed. Gather the lace and sew it around the seam line, adjusting the gathers evenly. On the back of the sachet a double layer of net will be visible due to the transparency of the fabric; stitch the lace braid over this to hide it. Fold the ribbons in half and sew in a loop to the back of the sachet. Trim the front at the top in the centre with a bow of cream ribbon. The sachet can be hung from a hook or a clothes-hanger, or can be placed in a drawer to scent the contents.

| DESIGN 22 | | |
|---|---|---|
| ANCHOR | | DMC |
| 0403 | ■ | 310 |
| 077 | ■ | 602 |
| 089 | ■ | 917 |
| 0134 | ■ | 820 |
| 09046 | ■ | 321 |
| 0101 | ■ | 550 |
| BACK STITCH | | |
| 0403 | – | 310 |
| 0923 | – | 699 |

# MOTHER'S DAY GREETING

Stitch on cream Zweigart 'Linda', 27 threads to 1in (2.5cm).
Finished size – 6×4½in (15.2×11.4cm).
Cut fabric to fit an 8in (20cm) embroidery hoop.

## TO MOUNT
Follow the mounting instructions (Method 2) on p123.
*You will need:*
☐ White card – 8¼×14in (20.9×35.6cm) to make a top-folded card
☐ White backing card – 8¼×7in (20.9×17.8cm)
☐ Window template – 62 squares × 50, cut from graph paper which has 10 squares to 1in (2.5cm)

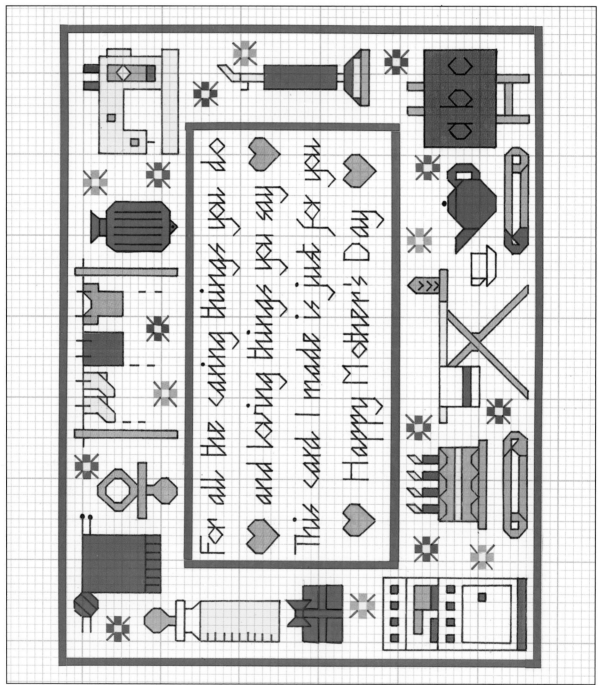

**DESIGN 23**

TO TRIM
1yd (1m) each of Offray Rose Pink (154) and Rosewood (169) 3mm ribbon
4 pink flower beads and 2 leaf beads (optional)

Punch two holes in the left-hand side of the card. Thread the ribbons through the holes and tie in a bow. Trim the ends of the ribbons to length and thread on the flower and leaf beads if used (Fig 47).

# FATHER'S DAY

Stitch on white deluxe Hardanger, Zweigart 'Oslo', 22 blocks to 1in (2.5cm).
Finished size – 2½×3¾in (6.3×9.5cm).
Cut fabric to fit a 6in (15cm) embroidery hoop. When the embroidery is complete, sew a small pearl button to each point of the collar to look like shirt buttons.

TO MOUNT
*You will need:*
☐ White card – 3½×5in (8.9×12.7cm)
☐ White backing card – 3½×5in (8.9×12.7cm)
☐ Window template – 25 squares × 38, cut from graph paper which has 10 squares to 1in (2.5cm)

This design is mounted in the style of a post card, rather than a folding card, because the tie tack fastener protrudes out the back. Follow the mounting instructions (Method 2) on p123, but do not score and fold the card. Instead, sandwich the embroidery between the two pieces of card. For the final touch, push the point of a small tie tack through all the layers and secure at the back with the tack fastener.

DESIGN 24

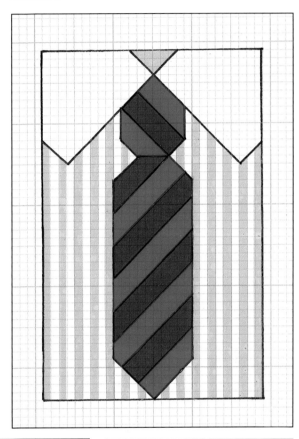

| DESIGN 23 | | | | | | |
|---|---|---|---|---|---|---|
| ANCHOR | | DMC | | ANCHOR | | DMC |
| 0243 | ■ | 989 | | 0400 | ■ | 413 |
| 09046 | ■ | 321 | | 01 | ☐ | blanc |
| 075 | ▨ | 604 | | BACK STITCH | | |
| 0300 | ☐ | 745 | | 0403 | – | 310 |
| 098 | ■ | 553 | | 0243 | – | 989 |
| 0131 | ▨ | 798 | | FRENCH KNOTS | | |
| 0890 | ▨ | 729 | | 0403 | ● | 310 |
| 0398 | ▨ | 415 | | | | |

| DESIGN 24 | | |
|---|---|---|
| ANCHOR | | DMC |
| 01 | ☐ | blanc |
| 0129 | ▨ | 809 |
| 0133 | ■ | 796 |
| 047 | ■ | 498 |
| BACK STITCH | | |
| 0403 | – | 310 |

# 4th July

# UNCLE SAM

Three cheers for the red, white and blue.
Celebrate the American sentiments of liberty and
freedom by working one of these projects for
Independence Day.

Stitch on white Zweigart 'Linda', 27 threads to
1in (2.5cm).
Finished size – 2¼×3½in (5.7×8.9cm).
Cut fabric to fit a 5in (13cm) embroidery hoop.

TO MOUNT
Follow the mounting instructions (Method 3) on
p124.
*You will need:*
☐ Red card – 9×6in (22.9×15.2cm) to make a
side-folded card
☐ White base card – 2¼×3½in (5.7×8.9cm)
☐ Wadding – 2¼×3½in (5.7×8.9cm)
☐ 1yd (1m) each of Offray White (029), Red
(250) and Royal Blue (350) 1.5mm ribbon, tied in
a bow around the card and trimmed to length

**DESIGN 25**

| ANCHOR | | DMC |
|---|---|---|
| 046 | ■ | 666 |
| 0133 | ■ | 796 |
| 01 | □ | blanc |
| 0403 | ■ | 310 |
| 06 | ■ | 754 |
| 09 | ■ | 760 |
| **BACK STITCH** | | |
| 0403 | – | 310 |
| **FRENCH KNOTS** | | |
| 0403 | ● | 310 |

DESIGN 25

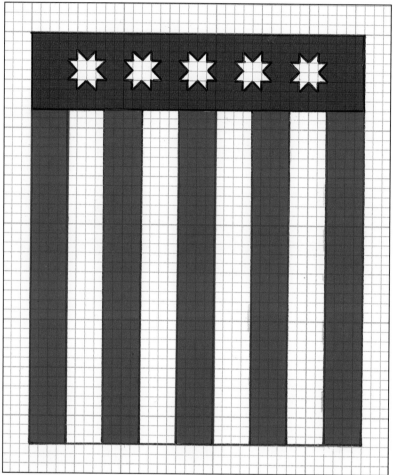

**DESIGN 26**

| DESIGN 26, 27 | | |
|---|---|---|
| ANCHOR | | DMC |
| 046 | ■ | 666 |
| 01 | □ | blanc |
| 0133 | ■ | 796 |
| 0403 | ■ | 310 |
| 0310 | ■ | 434 |
| 0217 | ■ | 319 |
| 0891 | ▢ | 676 |
| BACK STITCH | | |
| 0403 | – | 310 |

# JELLY BEAN BAG

Stitch on white deluxe Hardanger, Zweigart 'Oslo', 22 blocks to 1in (2.5cm).
Finished size – 3¼×3¾in (8.2×9.5cm).
Cut fabric 4¼×9½in (11×24cm).
Fold the fabric in half – 4¼×4¾in (11×12cm) – and embroider the bottom of the design centrally, one thread up from the fold. The white stars and stripes need not be embroidered; they can be left as bare fabric.

TO MAKE UP
Follow the instructions for making a tote bag on p124, but make the handle by sewing 1yd (1m) of dark blue piping cord to the sides of the bag as shown on p44. Knot and then fray the ends of the cord.

46

**DESIGN 27**

# BALD EAGLE

Stitch on white deluxe Hardanger, Zweigart
'Oslo', 22 blocks to 1in (2.5cm).
Finished size – 5×4½in (12.7×11.4cm).
Cut fabric to fit an 8in (20cm) embroidery hoop.

## TO MOUNT
Follow the mounting instructions (Method 2) on
p123.

*You will need:*
☐ Dark blue card – 8×15in (20.3×38cm) to
make a top-folded card
☐ White backing card – 8×7½in (20.3×19cm)
☐ Window template – 53 squares × 48, cut from
graph paper which has 10 squares to 1in (2.5cm)

## TO TRIM
Stick a white sticky paper star at each corner of
the window. (Gold stars are more readily available
and are usually white on the reverse.)

# Hallowe'en

# WICKED WITCH

Stitch on cream deluxe Hardanger, Zweigart 'Oslo', 22 blocks to 1in (2.5cm).
Finished size – 3½×3¼in (8.9× 8.2cm).
Cut fabric to fit a 5in (13cm) embroidery hoop.

## TO MOUNT
Follow the mounting instructions (Method 2) on p123.
*You will need:*
☐ Black card – 6½×14½in (16.5×36cm) to make a top-folded card
☐ White backing card – 6½× 7¼in (16.5×18cm)
☐ Window template – 40 squares × 40, cut from graph paper which has 10 squares to 1in (2.5cm)

| DESIGN 28, 29 | | |
|---|---|---|
| ANCHOR | | DMC |
| 0403 | ■ | 310 |
| 0400 | ▨ | 413 |
| 0234 | ☐ | 3072 |
| 0925 | ▨ | 970 |
| 0358 | ■ | 433 |
| 0260 | ☐ | 369 |
| 0290 | ▨ | 973 |
| 01 | ☐ | blanc |
| BACK STITCH | | |
| 0403 | – | 310 |
| FRENCH KNOTS | | |
| 0403 | ● | 310 |

## TO TRIM
*You will need:*
☐ 1yd (1m) Offray Torrid Orange (750) 1.5mm ribbon
☐ 12 gold and silver sticky stars

Stick the stars at random on the card. Tie the ribbon in a bow around the fold and trim the ends to length.

**DESIGN 28**

# TRICK-OR-TREAT BAG

Stitch on black Zweigart 'Linda', 27 threads to 1in (2.5cm).
Finished size – embroidery, 3× 2in (7.6×5.1cm); bag, 6×6in (15.2×15.2cm).
Cut fabric 7×14in (17.8× 35.6cm).
Fold the fabric in half – 7×7in (17.8×17.8cm) – and embroider the bottom of the design centrally 2in (5cm) up from fold.

## TO MAKE UP
Follow the instructions for making a tote bag given on p124.
Make two handles from 24in (61cm) grosgrain ribbon 1in (2.5cm) wide, cut into 2 × 12in (30.5cm) lengths. Neaten the ends of the ribbon and sew the handles to the bag. For added effect, an orange bead with pumpkin features drawn in felt-tip pen can be attached to a handle using orange, white and black ribbon.

**DESIGN 29**

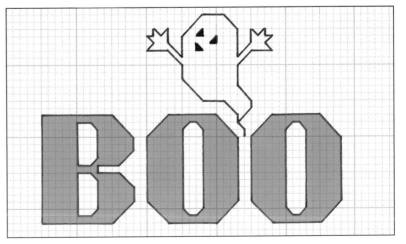

# Harvest and Thanksgiving

DESIGN 30

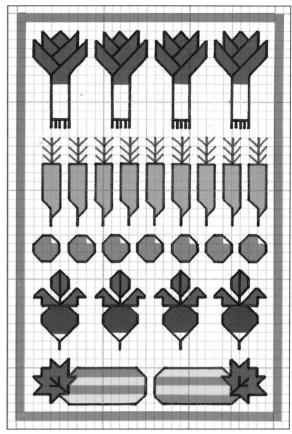

DESIGN 31

# FRUITS OF THE EARTH

Stitch on cream deluxe Hardanger, Zweigart 'Oslo', 22 blocks to 1in (2.5cm).
Finished size – 2¾×4in (7 × 10.2cm).
Cut fabric to fit a 6in (15cm) embroidery hoop.

TO MOUNT
Follow the mounting instructions (Method 2) on p123.
*You will need:*
☐ Green card – 9×6in (23× 15.2cm) to make a side-folded card
☐ White backing card – 4½× 6in (11.5×15.2cm)
☐ Window template – 31 squares × 44, cut from graph paper which has 10 squares to 1in (2.5cm)

| DESIGN 30, 31 | | | | | |
|---|---|---|---|---|---|
| ANCHOR | | DMC | ANCHOR | | DMC |
| 0226 | ▧ | 702 | 098 | ▨ | 553 |
| 0923 | ▦ | 699 | 01 | ☐ | blanc |
| 0290 | ▧ | 973 | 0403 | ■ | 310 |
| 0307 | ▦ | 783 | **FRENCH KNOTS** | | |
| 0925 | ▨ | 947 | 0403 | ● | 310 |
| 046 | ▦ | 666 | **BACK STITCH** | | |
| 0799 | ▦ | 498 | 0403 | – | 310 |

# Birthdays

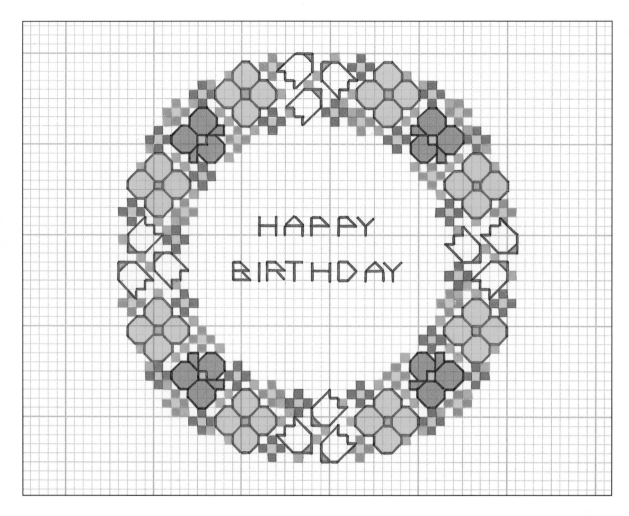

# SPRING BIRTHDAY

Stitch on cream Zweigart 'Linda', 27 threads to 1in (2.5cm).
Finished size – 3½in (8.9cm) diameter circle.
Cut fabric to fit a 5in (13cm) embroidery hoop.

TO MOUNT
Follow the mounting instructions (Method 1) on p122.
*You will need:*
☐ 1 white ready-made card mount with a 3¾in (9.5cm) diameter circular window

This design has also been mounted in the lid of a Framecraft 4in (10.2cm) porcelain bowl (see p36). Mount as recommended by the manufacturer. To adapt this design for use at Easter, substitute the greeting 'Happy Easter', using the alphabet (Fig 18) on p116 and the design instructions on p119.

| DESIGN 32 | | | | | |
|---|---|---|---|---|---|
| ANCHOR | | DMC | ANCHOR | | DMC |
| 0204 | ☐ | 913 | 0131 | ■ | 798 |
| 0295 | ☐ | 726 | **BACK STITCH** | | |
| 0109 | ☐ | 209 | 0862 | — | 520 |
| 01 | ☐ | blanc | 0101 | — | 550 |
| 074 | ☐ | 3689 | | | |

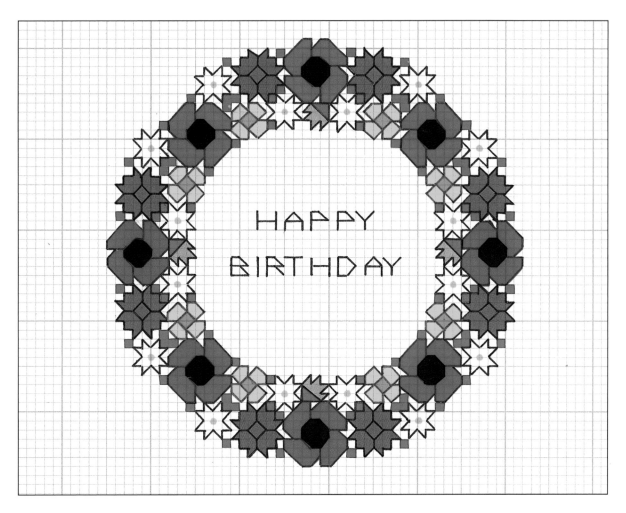

# SUMMER BIRTHDAY

Stitch on cream Zweigart 'Linda', 27 threads to 1in (2.5cm).
Finished size – 3½in (8.9cm) diameter circle.
Cut fabric to fit a 5in (13cm) embroidery hoop.

TO MOUNT
Follow the mounting instructions (Method 1) on p122.
*You will need:*
☐ 1 white ready-made card mount with a 3¾in (9.5cm) diameter circular window

| DESIGN 33 | | | | | |
|---|---|---|---|---|---|
| ANCHOR | | DMC | ANCHOR | | DMC |
| 0228 | ■ | 701 | 099 | ■ | 552 |
| 046 | ■ | 666 | 076 | ▢ | 603 |
| 0403 | ■ | 310 | **BACK STITCH** | | |
| 01 | ☐ | blanc | 0403 | — | 310 |
| 0307 | ■ | 783 | **FRENCH KNOTS** | | |
| 0305 | ▢ | 743 | 0305 | ● | 743 |
| 0137 | ■ | 792 | | | |

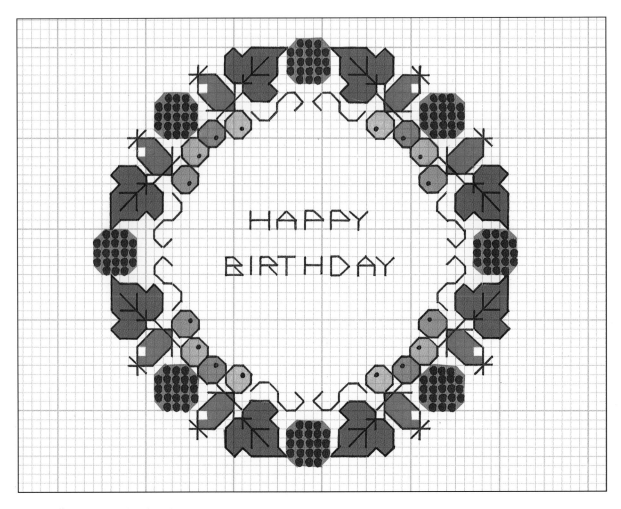

# AUTUMN BIRTHDAY

Stitch on cream Zweigart 'Linda', 27 threads to 1in (2.5cm).
Finished size – 3½in (8.9cm) diameter circle.
Cut fabric to fit a 5in (13cm) embroidery hoop.

The blackberries are worked using large French knots to give a raised, berry-like texture. To simulate the shine on the berries, two different colours of thread are combined in the needle.

TO MOUNT
Follow the mounting instructions (Method 1) on p122.
*You will need:*
☐ 1 white ready-made card mount with a 3¾in (9.5cm) diameter circular window

This design has been used also as a fiftieth birthday card on p59, by adding the number 50

| DESIGN 34 | | | | | |
|---|---|---|---|---|---|
| ANCHOR | | DMC | ANCHOR | | DMC |
| 01 | ☐ | blanc | 0326 | ■ | 900 |
| 0349 | ■ | 301 | **BACK STITCH** | | |
| 011 | ■ | 350 | 0269 | – | 935 |
| 0269 | ■ | 935 | **FRENCH KNOTS** | | |
| 0278 | ☐ | 734 | 0269 | ● | 935 |
| 0280 | ■ | 581 | **1 Strand** | | |
| | | | 0871 | ■ | 3041 |
| 0313 | ☐ | 977 | **2 Strands** | | |
| | | | 0152 | | 939 |

(Fig 17) on p116. A retirement card could be produced by changing the greeting. To alter the design, read the instructions on p119.

# WINTER BIRTHDAY

Stitch on cream Zweigart 'Linda', 27 threads to 1in (2.5cm).
Finished size – 3½in (8.9cm) diameter circle.
Cut fabric to fit a 5in (13cm) embroidery hoop.

TO MOUNT
Follow the mounting instructions (Method 1) on p122.
*You will need:*
☐ 1 white ready-made card mount with a 3¾in (9.5cm) diameter circular window

To alter this design to a Christmas card (shown on p9) change the greeting using the alphabet (Fig 18) on p116 and the design instructions on p119.

| DESIGN 35 | | | | | |
|---|---|---|---|---|---|
| ANCHOR | | DMC | ANCHOR | | DMC |
| 09046 | ■ | 321 | 0923 | ■ | 699 |
| 0288 | □ | 445 | **BACK STITCH** | | |
| 01 | □ | blanc | 0403 | – | 310 |
| 0371 | ■ | 433 | 0923 | – | 699 |
| 0225 | ■ | 703 | **FRENCH KNOTS** | | |
| 0228 | ■ | 701 | 0225 | ● | 703 |

# Special Birthdays

# BABY'S FIRST BIRTHDAY

Stitch on cream deluxe Hardanger, Zweigart 'Oslo', 22 blocks to 1in (2.5cm).
Finished size – 1½×2½in (3.8× 6.3cm).
Cut fabric to fit a 4in (10cm) embroidery hoop.

## TO MOUNT
Follow the mounting instructions (Method 1) on p122.
*You will need:*
☐ 1 pink or blue ready-made card mount with a 3in (7.6cm) oval window

## TO TRIM
*You will need:*
☐ ½yd (50cm) narrow lace trimming (choose a lace which lies well in an oval shape without buckling on the curves)
☐ UHU glue

DESIGN 36

| DESIGN 36 | | |
|---|---|---|
| ANCHOR | | DMC |
| 0300 | ☐ | 745 |
| 0890 | ◩ | 729 |
| 0978 | ◼ | 322 |
| 0976 | ◩ | 3325 |
| 0261 | ◩ | 966 |
| 077 | ◩ | 335 |
| 075 | ◩ | 3326 |
| **BACK STITCH** | | |
| 0400 | – | 317 |
| **FRENCH KNOTS** | | |
| 0400 | ● | 317 |

Glue the lace in place around the window, taking care to make a tidy join.

| DESIGN 37 | | |
|---|---|---|
| ANCHOR | | DMC |
| 01 | ☐ | blanc |
| 0403 | ◼ | 310 |
| 051 | ◩ | 604 |
| 0288 | ☐ | 445 |
| 0313 | ◩ | 977 |
| 0371 | ◼ | 433 |
| **FRENCH KNOTS** | | |
| 0129 | ◉ | 809 |
| 051 | ◉ | 604 |
| **BACK STITCH** | | |
| 0403 | – | 310 |

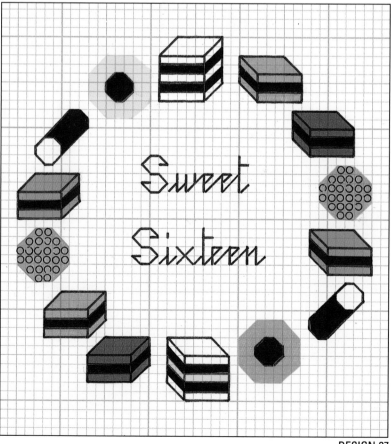

DESIGN 37

# SWEET SIXTEEN

For the eagle-eyed needleworker only, this design is stitched on a Framecraft Jar Lacy.

Finished size – 2¼in (5.7cm) diameter circle. Alternatively, stitch the design on a coarser fabric such as Zweigart 'Oslo' and mount it as a card.

## TO TRIM
*You will need:*
☐ 1yd (1m) each of Offray Lemon (640), White (029), Blue Mist (311) and Sable (843) 1.5mm ribbon

Thread the ribbons through the holes in the Jar Lacy. Fill a screw-top jar with liquorice allsorts and place the Jar Lacy over the lid. Pull the ribbons up tight, tie a bow and trim the ends of the ribbons to length.

# EIGHTEEN AND TWENTY ONE

Stitch the door on cream deluxe Hardanger, Zweigart 'Oslo', 22 blocks to 1in (2.5cm). Finished size – 2×4½in (5.1× 11.4cm). Cut fabric to fit a 6in (15cm) embroidery hoop. Stitch the numbers on cream Zweigart 'Linda', 27 threads to 1in (2.5cm). Finished size – 1×1in (2.5× 2.5cm). Cut fabric to fit a 2½in (6cm) embroidery hoop.

## TO MOUNT
Follow the mounting instructions (Method 3) p124.

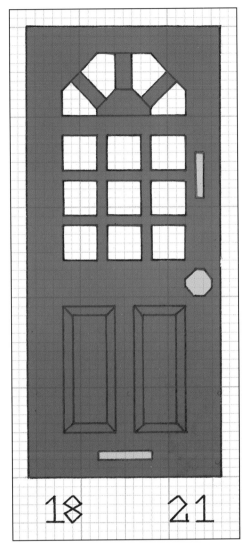

**DESIGN 38**

| DESIGN 38 | | |
|---|---|---|
| ANCHOR | | DMC |
| 047 | ■ | 498 |
| 0306 | ▫ | 783 |
| 0403 | ▦ | 310 |
| **BACK STITCH** | | |
| 0403 | – | 310 |

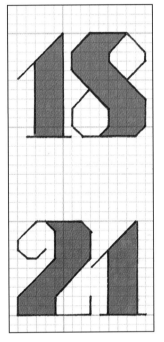

*You will need:*
☐ Gold card – 7×14in (17.8× 35.6cm) to make a top-folded card
☐ White card – 6×6in (15.2× 15.2cm), glued to the front of the scored and folded gold card
☐ White base card – 2×4½in (5.1×11.4cm)
☐ Wadding – 2×4½in (5.1× 11.4cm)
☐ UHU glue

## TO TRIM
*You will need:*
☐ 1–1¼in (3.2cm) key ring mount
☐ 1 door key
☐ ½yd (50cm) each of red, yellow and white 1.5mm ribbon

Mount the numbers in the key ring, following the manufacturer's instructions. Add to the key ring a shiny key and a bow made from the ribbons. Glue the padded and mounted door on the right-hand side of the card. Glue the key ring on the left-hand side and add a message in your own handwriting, or cut a greeting from an old card.
To greet the return of a prodigal child, mount your house number in the key ring and change the greeting to 'Welcome Home'.

# FORTY

Stitch on cream deluxe Hardanger, Zweigart 'Oslo', 22 blocks to 1in (2.5cm).
Finished size – 4¼×3in (10.8× 7.6cm).
Cut fabric to fit a 6in (15cm) embroidery hoop.

As you stitch, add one bead per row along the beading line indicated on the chart, following the instructions on p122 (Fig 32). The roses can be worked either in cross stitch or using bullion bars (Fig 31b).

TO MOUNT
Follow the mounting instructions (Method 1) on p122.

| DESIGN 39 | | |
|---|---|---|
| ANCHOR | | DMC |
| 0920 | ■ | 932 |
| 09 | ■ | 352 |
| 06 | ■ | 353 |
| 0301 | □ | 744 |
| 0214 | ■ | 368 |
| 0386 | □ | 746 |
| BACK STITCH (Flowers) | | |
| 09 | – | 352 |
| FRENCH KNOTS | | |
| 0301 | ● | 744 |
| BEADING LINE | | |
| | ▣ | |
| BACK STITCH (Numbers) | | |
| 0922 | – | 930 |

| DESIGN 40 | | | | | |
|---|---|---|---|---|---|
| ANCHOR | | DMC | ANCHOR | | DMC |
| 0920 | ■ | 932 | 0386 | □ | 746 |
| 0301 | ■ | 744 | BACK STITCH | | |
| 0214 | ■ | 368 | 069 | – | 3687 |
| 066 | ■ | 3689 | FRENCH KNOTS | | |
| 068 | ■ | 3688 | 0301 | ● | 744 |

*You will need:*
□ 1 white Framecraft CraftaCard with a window 5½× 3¾in (14×9.5cm)

TO TRIM
*You will need:*
□ 1yd (1m) eyelet lace 1½in (3.8cm) wide
□ 1yd (1m) Offray Coral Ice (205) 3mm ribbon
□ 4 apricot braid flower trims

Thread the ribbon through the holes in the eyelet lace. Starting and ending in a corner to hide the raw ends, glue the lace around the outside edge of the card. At each corner, mitre the lace so that it lies flat. Glue a braid flower trim to each corner.

# SIXTY

Stitch on cream Zweigart 'Linda', 27 threads to 1in (2.5cm).
Finished size – 2½×2¼in (6.3× 5.7cm).
Cut fabric to fit a 4in (10cm) embroidery hoop.

TO MOUNT
*You will need:*
□ 1 Framecraft heart-shaped porcelain box – 2½×2¼in (6.3×5.7cm)

Follow the manufacturer's instructions to mount the embroidery into the box.

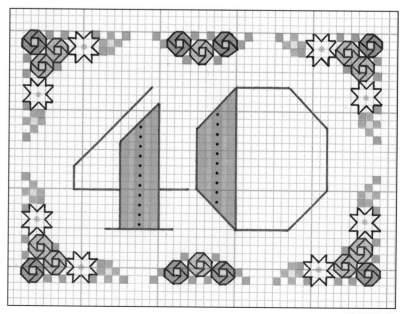

DESIGN 39

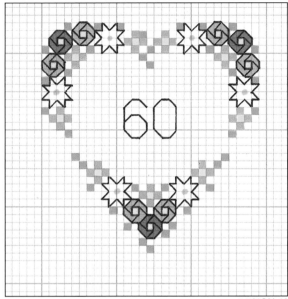

DESIGN 40

# SEVENTY

Stitch on cream deluxe Hardanger, Zweigart 'Oslo', 22 blocks to 1in (2.5cm).
Finished size – 3¼in (8.2cm) diameter circle.
Cut fabric to fit a 5in (13cm) embroidery hoop.

As you stitch, add one bead per row along the beading line indicated on the chart, following the

instructions on p122 (Fig 32). The roses can be worked either in cross stitch or using bullion bars (Fig 31b).

TO MOUNT
Follow the mounting instructions (Method 1) on p122.
*You will need:*
☐ 1 white ready-made card mount with a 3¾in (9.5cm) diameter circular window

TO TRIM
*You will need:*
☐ ½yd (50cm) narrow cream lace edging
☐ 1 ready-made cream pearl-trimmed bow
☐ UHU glue

Glue the lace around the window and cover the join at the bottom with the bow.

The numbers 0–9 are given on p117 (Fig 20) so that you can celebrate any birthday with your own design of card. Following the design instructions on p119, any numbers can be put together. For a rectangular-shaped card, surround the numbers with the border on the 40th birthday card opposite. The border is adjustable to fit any numbers you choose; just leave larger or smaller gaps between the components of the border. For a circular design use the curved floral designs on the 70th birthday card below.

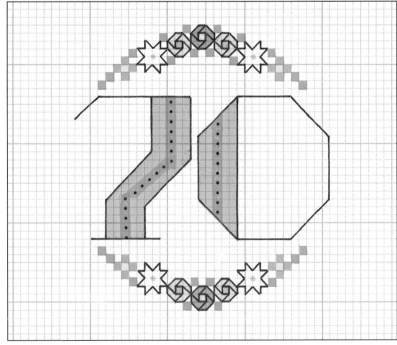

DESIGN 41

| DESIGN 41 | | |
|---|---|---|
| ANCHOR | | DMC |
| 0920 | ▨ | 932 |
| 0301 | ☐ | 744 |
| 0890 | ▨ | 676 |
| 0313 | ▨ | 977 |
| 0214 | ▨ | 368 |
| 0386 | ☐ | 746 |
| **BACK STITCH** | | |
| 0901 | – | 680 |
| **FRENCH KNOTS** | | |
| 0301 | ● | 744 |
| **BEADING LINE** | | |
| | ⊡ | |

DESIGN 41

# Marriage

# ENGAGEMENT CONGRATULATIONS

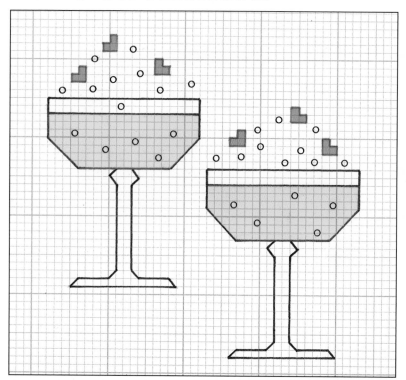

| DESIGN 42 | | |
|---|---|---|
| **ANCHOR** | | **DMC** |
| 0300 | ☐ | 745 |
| 066 | ◻ | 3688 |
| **BACK STITCH** | | |
| 0400 | — | 645 |
| 068 | — | 3687 |
| **SMALL GOLD BEADS** | | |
| | ○ | |

| DESIGN 43 | | |
|---|---|---|
| **ANCHOR** | | **DMC** |
| 0214 | ☐ | 368 |
| 0117 | ☐ | 341 |
| 096 | ◻ | 554 |
| 068 | ◼ | 3687 |
| 066 | ◻ | 3688 |
| 0301 | ☐ | 744 |
| **BACK STITCH** | | |
| 0217 | — | 319 |
| **FRENCH KNOTS** | | |
| 0214 | ● | 368 |
| 0117 | ● | 341 |
| 096 | ● | 554 |
| 0301 | ● | 744 |
| 068 | ● | 3687 |

DESIGN 42

Give a bottle of bubbly to celebrate an engagement and tie on a bottle collar for extra fizz.

Stitch on cream deluxe Hardanger, Zweigart 'Oslo', 22 blocks to 1in (2.5cm). Finished size – embroidery, 3½×3¾in (8.9×9.5cm); collar, 5½×11in (14×28cm). Cut fabric 7½×13in (19× 33cm).
Space has been left for you to add two names if you wish. Use the alphabet (Fig 14) on p115 and follow the design instructions on p119.

TO MAKE UP
*You will need:*
☐ 30 small gold beads to simulate bubbles
☐ 1½yd (1.5m) gold Russian braid
☐ Invisible nylon sewing thread
☐ White sewing thread

Sew the beads on using the invisible nylon thread (Fig 33b). Turn the raw edges of the fabric under ½in (1.5cm) to the back, then again another ½in (1.5cm) to hide all raw edges. Machine stitch the turnings. Cut the braid in half. Lay a piece of braid over the top and the bottom hemming lines on the right side of the fabric, matching the centre of the collar to the centre of the braid, and stitch the braid in place. The ends of the braid will protrude over the end of the collar and are left loose (Fig 5). Tie the loose ends of the braid in bows at the back of the bottle and trim to length.

**Fig 5** *Making up a bottle collar*

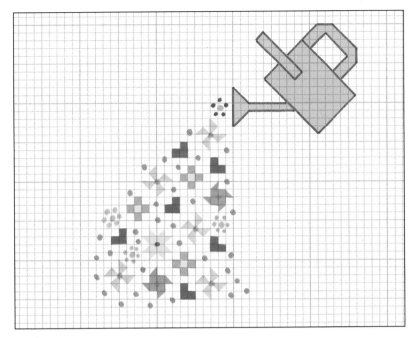

DESIGN 43

DESIGN 44

# BRIDAL SHOWER

Stitch on cream deluxe Hardanger, Zweigart 'Oslo', 22 blocks to 1in (2.5cm).
Finished size – 3¼×3¼in (8.2× 8.2cm).
Cut fabric to fit a 5in (13cm) embroidery hoop.

TO MOUNT
Follow the mounting instructions (Method 2) on p123.
*You will need:*
☐ White card – 11×6½in (28× 16.5cm) to make a side-folded card
☐ White backing card – 5½× 6½in (14×16.5cm)
☐ Window template – 36 squares × 36, cut from graph paper which has 10 squares to 1in (2.5cm)

Trim the card with 1yd (1m) Berisfords pale green (80) 3mm ribbon. Tie a bow around the fold and trim the ends of the ribbon to length.

# RICE SACK

This little sack of rice, decorated with a sweep, combines two traditions in one – rice is a traditional gift for the bridal couple, often thrown instead of confetti, and the presence of a sweep at a wedding is supposed to ensure good luck.

Stitch on cream deluxe Hardanger, Zweigart 'Oslo', 22 blocks to 1in (2.5cm).
Finished size – 1½×2½in (3.8× 6.3cm).
Cut fabric 14×4in (36×10cm). Fold the fabric in half, 7×4in (18×10cm) and stitch the bottom of the design centrally ¼in (6mm) up from the fold.

TO MAKE UP
Follow the instructions for making a tote bag on p124 but omit the handles. Fill the bag with rice and close it by tying firmly with ½yd (50cm) Offray White (029) 1.5mm ribbon. Tie a bow and trim the ends of the ribbon.

| DESIGN 44 | | |
|---|---|---|
| ANCHOR | | DMC |
| 0403 | ■ | 310 |
| 0233 | ■ | 451 |
| 01 | ☐ | blanc |
| 0357 | ■ | 975 |
| 09046 | ■ | 321 |
| 754 | ☐ | 06 |
| 760 | ☐ | 09 |
| BACK STITCH | | |
| 0403 | – | 310 |
| 0357 | – | 975 |
| FRENCH KNOTS | | |
| 0403 | ● | 310 |

# RING PILLOW

Take the rings to the church presented on this pillow and there will be no risk of the best man losing them.

Stitch on cream Zweigart 'Linda', 27 threads to 1in (2.5cm).
Finished size – embroidery, 3½×4½in (8.9× 11.4cm).
Cut a piece of 'Linda' 11×11in (28×28cm) and another similar piece for the backing.
Space has been left for you to add two names and a date if you so wish. Use the alphabet (Fig 14) on p115 and follow the design instructions on p119. When the embroidery is complete, sew on tiny beads (Fig 33a) as indicated on the chart.

## TO MAKE UP
*You will need:*
☐ 1–10in (25.4cm) cushion pad
☐ White sewing thread

Place the two pieces of 'Linda' right sides together and seam around allowing a ½in (1.5cm) seam allowance. Leave an opening in one side. Turn right side out, insert the cushion pad and slipstitch closed.

## TO TRIM
*You will need:*
☐ 8ft (2.5m) × 3in (7.6cm) cream lace edging
☐ 1½yd (1.5m) × 1¼in (3.2cm) eyelet lace
☐ 1½yd (1.5m) × 7mm cream ribbon
☐ 1yd (1m) × 1.5mm cream ribbon
☐ 5½yd (5.5m) × 1.5mm apricot ribbon
☐ Tiny cream, pale green and pink beads
☐ Ribbon roses – 4 cream, 2 apricot ▷

| DESIGN 45 | | |
|---|---|---|
| ANCHOR | | DMC |
| 0881 | ☐ | 945 |
| 0213 | ☐ | 369 |
| 01 | ☐ | blanc |
| **BACK STITCH** | | |
| 0850 | – | 926 |
| 09575 | – | 758 |
| 0848 | – | 928 |
| **FRENCH KNOTS** | | |
| 0850 | ● | 926 |
| **BEADS** | | |
| | ● | green |
| | ● | pink |
| | ● | cream |

DESIGN 45

Sew the ends of the lace edging together and neaten the raw edges. Gather the lace into a frill and, distributing all gathers evenly, sew it around the edge of the pillow 1in (2.5cm) in from the seam line. Thread the 7mm cream ribbon and then the 1.5mm apricot ribbon through the eyelet lace so that the apricot ribbon lies on top of the cream ribbon. Sew the eyelet lace over the edge of the lace frill to hide the gathered edge, mitreing the corners so that they lie flat. Sew a pink, green and cream bead at regular intervals along the ribbon line. Make 4 multi-looped bows of apricot ribbon (Fig 46) and sew one to each corner. Trim each bow by sewing on a cream ribbon rose. Cut the 1.5mm cream ribbon in half, fold each piece in half and attach on each side of the pillow as shown on p69. Sew the apricot ribbon roses at the top on the folds of cream ribbon. Tie the wedding rings to the cream ribbons, and to stop them rolling around, hold them temporarily in place with pins.

# CHURCH WEDDING

Stitch on cream Zweigart 'Linda', 27 threads to 1in (2.5cm).
Finished size – 2×4in (5.1× 10.2cm).
Cut fabric to fit a 5in (13cm) embroidery hoop.
Add initials to the centres of the garlands using the alphabet (Fig 13) on p115.

TO MOUNT
Follow the mounting instructions (Method 1) on p122.
*You will need:*
☐ 1 ready-made gothic window card mount – 4¼×6¼in (10.8× 15.9cm)

Trim the card by tying 1yd (1m) each of Offray Blue Mist (311) and White (029) 1.5mm ribbon in a bow around the card. Trim the ends of the ribbons to length. For an extra surprise include some confetti which will flutter out when the card is opened.

DESIGN 46

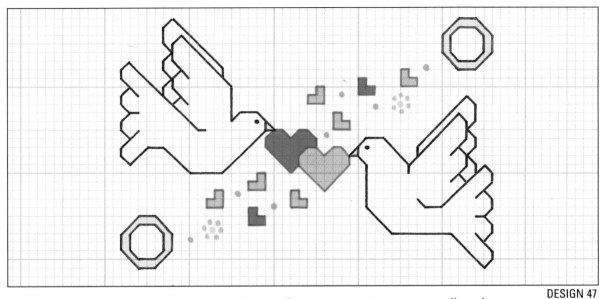

# REGISTRY OFFICE WEDDING

Stitch on cream deluxe Hardanger, Zweigart 'Oslo', 22 blocks to 1in (2.5cm). Finished size – 4×3in (10.2× 7.6cm).

Cut fabric to fit a 6in (15cm) embroidery hoop.
Space has been left for you to add two names if you wish. Use the alphabet (Fig 14) on p115 and follow the design instructions on p119.

TO MOUNT
Follow the mounting instructions (Method 1) on p122.

*You will need:*
☐ 1 white ready-made card mount with a window 5½× 3¾in (14×9.5cm)

For an extra surprise include some confetti which will flutter out when the card is opened.

| DESIGN 46 | | | | | |
|---|---|---|---|---|---|
| ANCHOR | | DMC | ANCHOR | | DMC |
| 01 | ☐ | blanc | **BACK STITCH** | | |
| 0234 | ☐ | 762 | 0400 | – | 317 |
| 0235 | ☐ | 414 | 010 | – | 3328 |
| 06 | ☐ | 754 | 0215 | – | 320 |
| 09 | ☐ | 760 | **FRENCH KNOTS** | | |
| 0146 | ☐ | 334 | 0144 | ● | 3325 |
| 0144 | ☐ | 3325 | 0301 | ● | 744 |
| 0215 | ☐ | 320 | 0215 | ● | 320 |
| 0301 | ☐ | 744 | 09 | ● | 760 |
| | | | 0400 | ● | 317 |

| DESIGN 47 | | |
|---|---|---|
| ANCHOR | | DMC |
| 01 | ☐ | blanc |
| 0295 | ☐ | 726 |
| 074 | ☐ | 3689 |
| 066 | ☐ | 3688 |
| **BACK STITCH** | | |
| 0400 | – | 317 |
| 068 | – | 3687 |
| **FRENCH KNOTS** | | |
| 0400 | ● | 317 |
| 0117 | ● | 341 |
| 0214 | ● | 368 |
| 0295 | ● | 726 |

# WEDDING ANNIVERSARIES 1–60

To make a card, stitch on cream deluxe Hardanger, Zweigart 'Oslo', 22 blocks to 1in (2.5cm). Finished size – 3½in (8.9cm) diameter circle.
Cut fabric to fit a 5in (13cm) embroidery hoop.
The chart for a Ruby anniversary is given here as a sample. If you are going to add a bow and trimmings, omit the greeting and the flowers in the centre of the design. Adapt the chart to suit other anniversaries by adding the number of the anniversary from the numbers (Fig 16) on p116. Add the name of the anniversary using the alphabet (Fig 19) on p116 and the design instructions on p119. No colour key is given because it is best to use colours to complement the occasion and the trimmings that you have chosen.

## TO MOUNT
Follow the mounting instructions (Method 1) on p122.
*You will need:*
☐ 1 ready-made card mount

with a 3¾in (9.5cm) diameter circular window

## TO TRIM
*You will need:*
☐ ½yd (50cm) 1.5mm ribbon
☐ Beads, or other appropriate trimmings

With the card lying flat, thread a length of ribbon through the fabric centrally, just below the bells. Thread or glue your chosen trimmings onto another length of ribbon, and place this over, and at right angles to, the first ribbon. Tie the first ribbon firmly in a knot thus anchoring the trimmings. Stand the card up and allow the trimmings to hang down. Now tie the loose ends of the first ribbon in a bow and trim the ends to length.

As an anniversary gift, work the design on 'Linda' and mount in the 4in (10.2cm) lid of a Framecraft lead crystal bowl (opposite), or a Framecraft musical box, which plays 'The Anniversary Waltz' (p75).

## SUGGESTIONS FOR TRIMMINGS

| | |
|---|---|
| *First* | Paper – paper flowers or petal-type confetti |
| *Second* | Cotton – miniature cotton reels or cotton thread wound around small card bobbins |
| *Third* | Leather – leather-look buttons |
| *Fourth* | Fruit – fruit-shaped beads or buttons |
| *Fifth* | Wood – wooden beads or buttons |
| *Sixth* | Sugar or candy – sugar cubes or sweets |
| *Seventh* | Wool – woollen pompons or a small toy sheep |
| *Eighth* | Bronze – coins |
| *Ninth* | Pottery – miniature pot or doll's house flower pot |
| *Tenth* | Tin – any tin-coloured shiny trinket or doll's house food tins |
| *Eleventh* | Steel – beads or darning needles |
| *Twelfth* | Silk – silk flowers or silk thread wound around small card bobbins |
| *Thirteenth* | Lace – miniature lace bobbins or guipure lace flower motifs |
| *Fourteenth* | Ivory – to save an elephant you could use an elephant pendant rather than anything made of ivory |
| *Fifteenth* | Crystal – clear faceted beads |
| *Twentieth* | China – beads or doll's house cups. |
| *Twenty-fifth* | Silver – silver charms, coins or rings |
| *Thirtieth* | Pearl – beads or buttons |
| *Thirty-fifth* | Coral – beads |
| *Fortieth* | Ruby – red faceted beads or a red heart pendant |
| *Forty-fifth* | Sapphire – blue faceted beads |
| *Fiftieth* | Gold – rings, beads or any golden trinkets |
| *Fifty-fifth* | Emerald – green faceted beads |
| *Sixtieth* | Diamond – glass faceted beads |

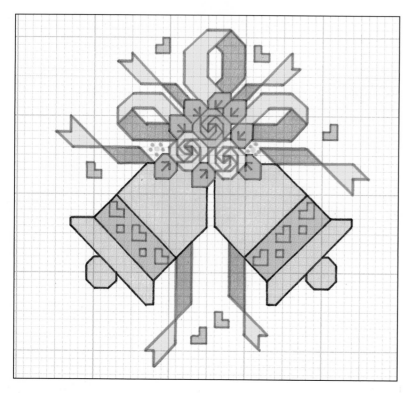

| DESIGN 49 | | |
|---|---|---|
| ANCHOR | | DMC |
| (0398) 0398 | ☐ | 415 (415) |
| (066) 0894 | ☐ | 224 (3688) |
| (01) | ☐ | Fil or mi-fin (blanc) |
| 0891 | ☐ | 677 |
| 0890 | ☐ | 729 |
| 0386 | ☐ | 746 |
| 0875 | ☐ | 503 |
| **BACK STITCH** | | |
| 0400 | – | 413 |
| (0400 + DMC Fil argent) | | (413 + Fil argent) |
| 0901 | – | 680 |
| (068) 0897 | – | 221 (3687) |
| 0879 | – | 500 |
| **FRENCH KNOTS** | | |
| 0894 | ● | 224 |
| 0891 | ● | 677 |

Thread numbers for "Silver Wedding" are given in brackets

# SILVER WEDDING

Stitch on cream deluxe Hardanger, Zweigart 'Oslo', 22 blocks to 1in (2.5cm).
Finished size – 3½×4½in (8.9×11.4cm).
Cut fabric to fit a 5in (13cm) embroidery hoop.
Embroider only the bells and hearts; the ribbons and roses are appliquéd later.

TO MOUNT
Follow the mounting instructions (Method 1) on p122.
*You will need:*
☐ 1 Framecraft CraftaCard with a 5½×3¾in (14×9.5cm) oval window

TO TRIM
*You will need:*
☐ Oddments of silver ribbon
☐ Ribbon roses – 1 white, 1 pink and 1 pale blue

☐ UHU glue

Cut short lengths of silver ribbon and fold to form loops. Glue the loops in place using the chart and the photograph opposite as a guide. Cut more short lengths of silver ribbon; trim the ends to points and glue these in place as indicated on the chart. Cover the raw edges of the loops by glueing ribbon roses over them. Glue lengths of ribbon to the card mount to form an extra frame.

# GOLDEN WEDDING

Stitch on cream Zweigart 'Linda', 27 threads to 1in (2.5cm).
Finished size – 3¼×3¼in (8.2×8.2cm).
Cut fabric to fit a 5in (13cm) embroidery hoop.

TO MOUNT
Follow the mounting instructions (Method 1) on p122.
*You will need:*
☐ 1 white ready-made card mount with a 3¾in (9.5cm) diameter circular window

TO TRIM
*You will need:*
☐ 1yd (1m) fine gold ribbon
☐ A bow made from gold parcel-wrapping ribbon
☐ 2 gold beads

Tie the fine gold ribbon around the card in a bow, catching the bow of parcel-wrapping ribbon in the process. Thread the two beads on to the ends of the fine ribbon (Fig 47) and trim the ends to length.

GOLD

HAPPY
ANNIVERSARY

50

# Babies

# BABY SHOWER

Present the mother-to-be with a
pretty and practical nappy
pincushion or cotton bud holder.
Alternatively, you could use this
design to make a card.

Stitch on cream deluxe
Hardanger, Zweigart 'Oslo', 22
blocks to 1in (2.5cm).
Finished size – 3×3in (7.6×
7.6cm).

Nappy pincushion:
Cut the fabric 5×5in (12.7×
12.7cm). When the embroidery
is complete, cut another piece of
fabric 5×5in (12.7×12.7cm)
and another, 2½×17in (6.3×

43cm). Take a ½in (1.5cm)
turning on each side of each
piece of fabric and tack the raw
edges to the back of the fabric.
Slipstitch the pieces together
(Fig 6), leaving an opening at the
back. Stuff firmly with Fibrefill
and slipstitch closed. Remove
the tacking threads and stitch
1yd (1m) of decorative piping
cord over the seams to cover
them.
Cotton bud holder:
Select a suitable tub of cotton
buds and cut a strip of fabric
large enough to go round it,
allowing an extra ½in (1.5cm)
all round for turnings.
Embroider the design centrally
on to this strip of fabric. When
the embroidery is complete, turn

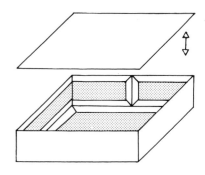

**Fig 6** *Making up a pincushion*

the raw edges to the wrong side
and stick them down with
Wundaweb bonding fleece.
Wrap the holder around the tub,
and joining the edges at the
back, slipstitch into place.

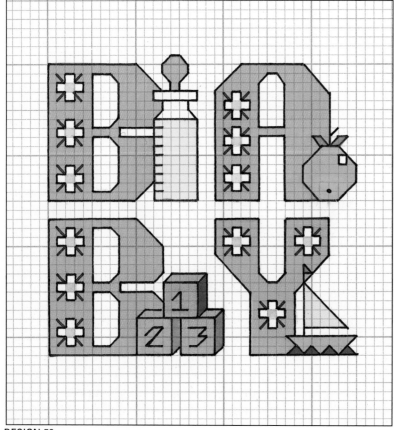

DESIGN 50

| DESIGN 50 | | |
|---|---|---|
| ANCHOR | | DMC |
| 075 | ▧ | 3326 |
| 077 | ▧ | 335 |
| 0976 | ▧ | 3325 |
| 0978 | ▧ | 322 |
| 0300 | ▧ | 745 |
| 0890 | ▧ | 729 |
| 0261 | ▧ | 966 |
| 0204 | ▧ | 913 |
| 01 | ☐ | blanc |
| BACK STITCH | | |
| 0400 | – | 317 |
| FRENCH KNOT | | |
| 0400 | ● | 317 |

DESIGN 51

# TWINS

Stitch on cream deluxe
Hardanger, Zweigart 'Oslo', 22
blocks to 1in (2.5cm).
Finished size – 3¾×4in (9.5×
10.2cm).
Cut fabric to fit a 6in (15cm)
embroidery hoop.

TO MOUNT
Follow the mounting
instructions (Method 2) on
p123.
*You will need:*
☐ White card covered with
mini-print paper – 7×14in
(17.8×35.6cm) to make a top-
folded card

☐ White backing card – 7×7in
(17.8×17.8cm)
☐ Window template – 42

squares × 45, cut from graph
paper which has 10 squares to
1in (2.5cm)

| DESIGN 51 | | | | | |
|---|---|---|---|---|---|
| ANCHOR | | DMC | ANCHOR | | DMC |
| 075 | ■ | 3326 | 0261 | ■ | 966 |
| 077 | ■ | 335 | 0234 | ■ | 3072 |
| 0976 | ■ | 3325 | 01 | ☐ | blanc |
| 0978 | ■ | 322 | **BACK STITCH** | | |
| 0300 | ■ | 745 | 0400 | – | 317 |
| 0890 | ■ | 729 | **FRENCH KNOTS** | | |
| | | | 0890 | ● | 729 |

# ROCK-A-BYE BABY

Stitch on cream Zweigart 'Linda', 27 threads to 1in (2.5cm).
Finished size – 3×3½in (7.6×8.9cm).
Cut fabric to fit a 5in (13cm) embroidery hoop. Space has been left for you to add a name, date and weight, if you wish. Use the numbers on this page, the alphabet on the opposite page and follow the design instructions on p119.

TO MOUNT
Follow the mounting instructions (Method 2) on p123.
*You will need:*
☐ White card covered with pale pink, mottled

writing paper – 10×6in (25.4×15.2cm) to make a side-folded card
☐ White backing card – 5×6in (12.7×15.2cm)
☐ Window template – 35 squares × 40, cut from graph paper which has 10 squares to 1in (2.5cm)

TO TRIM
*You will need:*
☐ 1yd (1m) Offray Rosewood (169) 1.5mm ribbon
☐ 2 pink heart beads (optional)

Tie the ribbon in a bow around the card and thread the beads on to the ends of the ribbon (Fig 47). Trim the ends to length.

| DESIGN 52 | | |
|---|---|---|
| ANCHOR | | DMC |
| 050 | ☐ | 605 |
| 076 | ▣ | 603 |
| 0292 | ☐ | 3078 |
| 0208 | ☐ | 563 |
| 0310 | ▣ | 434 |
| 0387 | ☐ | 712 |
| 01 | ☐ | blanc |
| 0108 | ▣ | 210 |
| 0977 | ☐ | 334 |
| 06 | ☐ | 754 |
| 09 | ☐ | 760 |
| **FRENCH KNOTS** | | |
| 0400 | ● | 413 |
| **BACK STITCH** | | |
| 0400 | – | 413 |
| 0208 | – | 563 |

# BOUNCING BABY

Stitch on cream Zweigart 'Linda', 27 threads to
1in (2.5cm).
Finished size – 3×3½in (7.6×8.9cm).
Cut fabric to fit a 6in (15cm) embroidery hoop.
Space has been left for you to add a name, if
you wish. Use the alphabet on this page and
follow the design instructions on p119.

## TO MOUNT
Follow the mounting instructions (Method 2) on
p123.
*You will need:*
☐ White card covered with pale blue, mottled
writing paper – 9×5½in (23×14cm) to make a
side-folded card

☐ White backing card – 4½×5½in (11.5×14cm)
☐ Window template – 32 squares × 37, cut from
graph paper which has 10 squares to 1in (2.5cm)

## TO TRIM
*You will need:*
☐ 1yd (1m) Offray Antique Blue (338) 1.5mm
ribbon
☐ 2 blue butterfly beads (optional)

Tie the ribbon in a bow around the card and
thread the beads onto the ends of the ribbon
(Fig 47). Trim the ends to length.

| DESIGN 53 | | |
|---|---|---|
| ANCHOR | | DMC |
| 0978 | ▨ | 322 |
| 0185 | ▨ | 964 |
| 0301 | ☐ | 744 |
| 075 | ▨ | 3326 |
| 01 | ☐ | blanc |
| 06 | ☐ | 754 |
| 09 | ▨ | 760 |
| FRENCH KNOTS | | |
| 0400 | ● | 413 |
| BACK STITCH | | |
| 0400 | – | 413 |

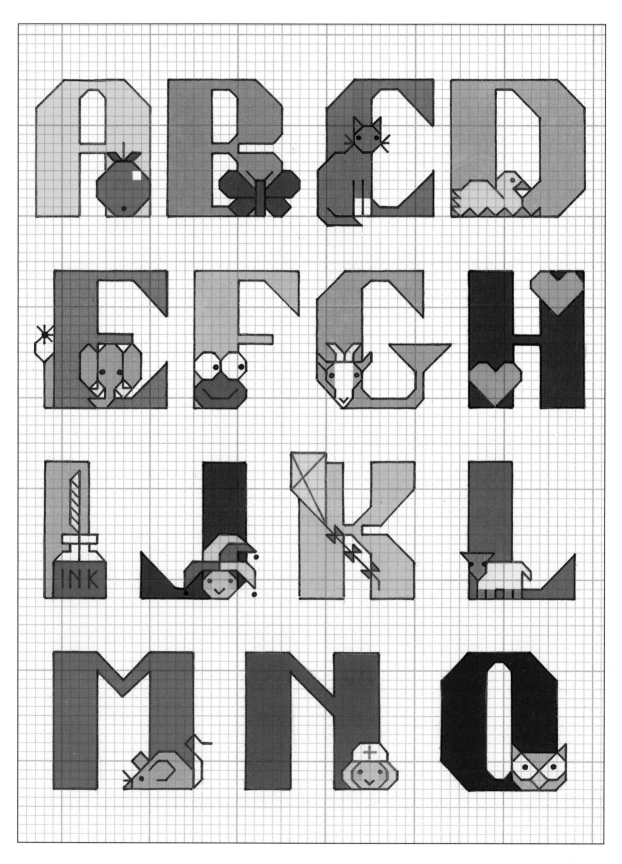

# NURSERY ALPHABET

This alphabet can be stitched to make a cheerful nursery wall decoration using colours of your choice; you could add a border or just stitch a line of cross stitches around it.

If letters are taken singly they can be used to personalise items for children, or a number of letters can be put together to spell out names. An initial in a tiny frame is a very acceptable gift, and is quick to produce. Names can be stitched directly on to suitable items such as a best bib and tucker on p77 or can be stitched on to evenweave ribbons ready to be appliquéd to garments or towels.

The design for the framed initials on p77 came from the alphabet (Fig 12, p114) combined with the border flowers from the fortieth birthday card on p62. To produce designs for the initials of your choice, follow the instructions on p119.

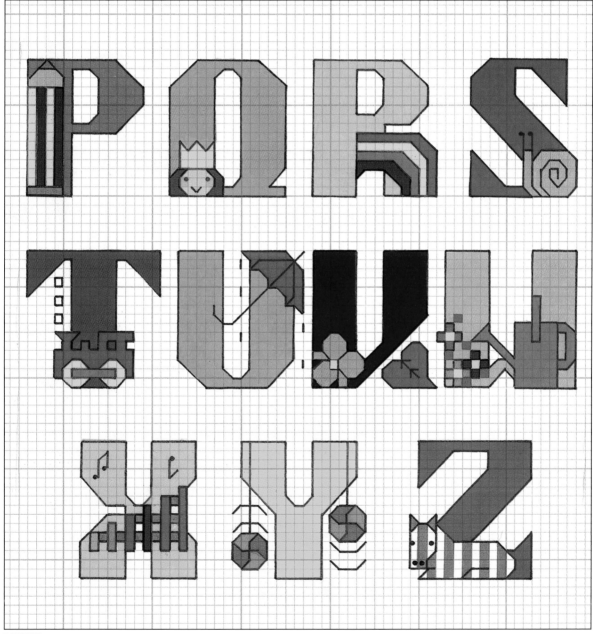

**DESIGN 54**

# CHRISTENING CANDLE

Stitch on cream Zweigart 'Linda', 27 threads to 1in (2.5cm).
Finished size – 2×3¾in (5.1×9.5cm).
Cut fabric to fit a 5in (13cm) embroidery hoop.

TO MOUNT
Follow the mounting instructions (Method 1) on p122.
*You will need:*
☐ 1 ready-made gothic window card mount – 4¼×6¼in (10.8×15.9cm)

# CHRISTENING RATTLE

A very special keepsake, though for reasons of safety, a baby or young child should not be allowed to play with the rattle, as the beads and bells could be chewed off and swallowed.

Stitch on cream Zweigart 'Linda', 27 threads to 1in (2.5cm).
Finished size of each motif – ¾×¾in (2×2cm).
Cut 12 pieces of fabric to fit a 4in (10cm) embroidery hoop. Work each of the four patterns on p86 (a, b, c, and d) three times.

| DESIGN 55 | | |
|---|---|---|
| ANCHOR | | DMC |
| 0300 | ☐ | 745 |
| 0301 | ☐ | 744 |
| 0297 | ▨ | 725 |
| – | ☐ | Fil or mi-fin |
| 0975 | ☐ | 775 |
| 0977 | ▨ | 334 |
| BACK STITCH | | |
| 0400 | — | 413 |
| 0102 | — | 550 |
| 068 | — | 3687 |
| – | — | Fil or mi-fin |
| FRENCH KNOTS | | |
| 0400 | ● | 413 |
| 068 | ● | 3687 |

DESIGN 55

Shine as a light in the world

IHS

## TO MAKE UP
*You will need:*
☐ 12 paper pentagons cut from Template 3 on p118
☐ Sewing cotton
☐ Fibrefill stuffing

Pin a paper pentagon to the wrong side of each embroidered motif, centreing the design and aligning one straight side with the grain of the fabric. Trim away the excess fabric leaving a ¼in (7mm) turning. Fold the turnings to the back and tack in place (Fig 7). Repeat for all twelve motifs. Following the diagram (Fig 8), slipstitch the motifs, right sides together to form a ball. Leave a small opening through which the ball is turned right side out. Stuff firmly with Fibrefill and slipstitch closed.

## TO TRIM
*You will need:*
☐ 6 claw or Noddy bells
☐ 20 gold beads
☐ Small, toning, pastel-coloured beads
☐ 1yd (1m) each of Offray White (029), Blue Mist (311), Rose Pink (154), Mint (530), Lemon (640) and Iris (477) 1.5mm ribbon

To cover each seam, trim with a line of small beads strung onto thread and stitched down at the corner of each motif. Add a gold bead at each corner for extra effect. Working with the six coloured ribbons divided into pairs, make a ribbon plait 12in (30.5cm) long. Overlap the ends, hold them in place with a few stitches to form a loop, then trim the ends. Sew the loop to the top of the ball. Sew the claw bells in a circle around the loop and cover all fixings with a multi-looped bow (Fig 46) formed from the remnants of the ribbons. Hang the rattle somewhere safe, where it can be seen and heard, but not touched by small hands.

**Fig 7** *Tacking paper to fabric for patchwork*

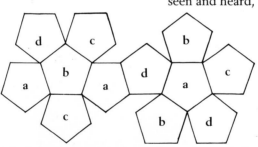

**Fig 8** *Sewing pentagons together to form a ball*

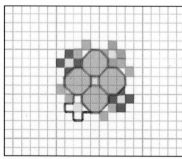

DESIGN 56A

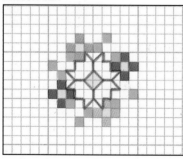

DESIGN 56B

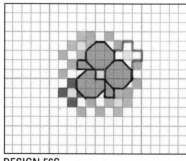

DESIGN 56C

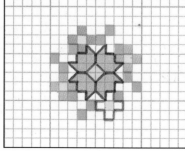

DESIGN 56D

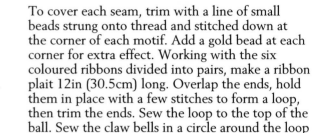

| DESIGN 56A, B, C, D | | |
|---|---|---|
| ANCHOR | | DMC |
| 0301 | ☐ | 744 |
| 066 | ▨ | 3688 |
| 0977 | ▧ | 334 |
| 0215 | ▨ | 320 |
| 01 | ☐ | blanc |
| 0109 | ▨ | 209 |
| 0975 | ▨ | 775 |
| BACK STITCH | | |
| 0102 | – | 550 |
| 068 | – | 3687 |
| 0132 | – | 797 |

# Religious Occasions

# BIBLE BOOKMARK

Stitch on white 'Aida', 18 blocks to 1in (2.5cm).
Finished size – 2¼×3in (5.7×7.6cm).
Cut fabric to fit a 4in (10cm) embroidery hoop.

TO MOUNT
*You will need:*
☐ 20in (51cm) Berisfords white satin 70mm
ribbon
☐ ½yd (50cm) fine gold braid
☐ Wundaweb bonding fleece
☐ UHU glue
☐ 1–3in (7.6cm) tassel made from DMC Fil or
clair (Fig 45)

**Fig 9** *Making
up a bookmark*

'I am Alpha and Omega, the
beginning and the end, the first
and the last.' (*The Revelation of
St John (22:13)*)

In order not to damage the fine paper pages of a
Bible, only one single thickness of ribbon should
be allowed to lie between the pages. The
embroidery therefore should be applied to the
ribbon and should hang below the pages. Turn the
top of the ribbon over ½in (1.5cm) and then
again another ½in (1.5cm). Use Wundaweb to
hold the hem in place so that no stitching is
visible on the ribbon. Make a similar hem at the
bottom, then stitch (a) to (b) to form a point
(Fig 9). Trim the embroidery to fit the ribbon and
apply to the ribbon a short distance above the
pointed end, using Wundaweb. Avoid flattening
the stitching by placing the work face down on a
terry towel when you apply the heat required to
activate the Wundaweb. Cover the raw edges of
the fabric with gold braid glued carefully in place.
Sew the tassel to the point of the bookmark.

**DESIGN 57**

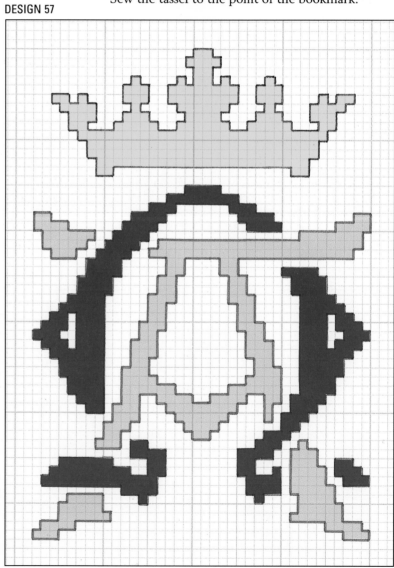

| DESIGN 57 | | |
|---|---|---|
| ANCHOR | | DMC |
| 0101 | ■ | 550 |
| 0204 | ▨ | 913 |
| 0306 | ▢ | 725 |
| **BACK STITCH** | | |
| | — | Fil or mi-fin |
| 0101 | — | 550 |
| 0923 | — | 699 |

# FIRST COMMUNION ROSARY PURSE

Stitch on cream Zweigart 'Linda', 27 threads to 1in (2.5cm).
Finished size – 1½×2½in (3.8×6.3cm).
Cut fabric 11×4in (28×10cm).
Embroider the top of the chalice centrally on the front of the purse 2½in (6.3cm) from the end of the fabric.

TO MAKE UP
Follow the instructions for making a purse on p125.
*You will need:*
☐ Cream silky lining fabric – 11×4in (28×10cm)
☐ 2 small gold buttons
☐ Scraps of gold Russian braid
☐ White sewing thread

# CONFIRMATION

Stitch on cream Zweigart 'Linda', 27 threads to 1in (2.5cm).
Finished size – 2½×2¼in (6.3×5.7cm).
Cut fabric to fit a 4in (10cm) embroidery hoop.
Space has been left for you to add a short name and a date if you wish. Use the alphabet (Fig 18) on p116 and follow the design instructions on p119.

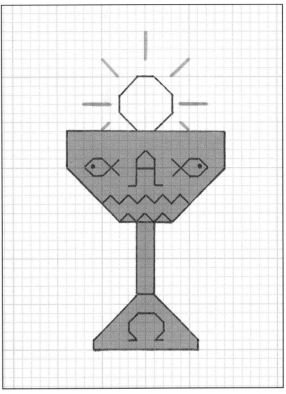

DESIGN 58

TO MOUNT
Follow the mounting instructions (Method 1) on p122.
*You will need:*
☐ 1 white, satin-finish, ready-made card mount with a 3¼in (8.2cm) diameter circular window

| DESIGN 58, 59 | | |
|---|---|---|
| ANCHOR | | DMC |
| 01 | ☐ | blanc |
| 0907 | ▣ | 833 |
| 0292 | ☐ | 3078 |
| | ▣ | Fil or mi-fin |
| 0117 | ☐ | 341 |
| BACK STITCH | | |
| 0400 | – | 645 |
| | – | Fil or mi-fin |

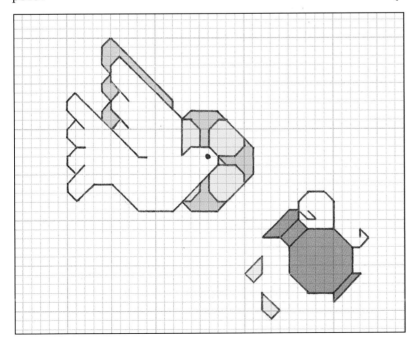

DESIGN 59

89

# FAITH, HOPE AND CHARITY

A bookmark for a prayer book or small Bible, depicting the cross (Faith), the anchor (Hope) and the heart (Charity).

Stitch on cream Zweigart 'Linda', 27 threads to 1in (2.5cm).
Finished size – 1¼×1½in (3.2×3.8cm).
Cut fabric to fit a 4in (10cm) embroidery hoop.

TO MOUNT
Follow the mounting instructions on p88.
*You will need:*
☐ 12in (30cm) Berisfords cream satin 38mm ribbon
☐ Wundaweb bonding fleece
☐ ¼yd (25cm) fine gold braid
☐ UHU glue
☐ 1–2in (5cm) tassel made from DMC Fil or clair (Fig 45)

# THE LORD IS MY SHEPHERD

Stitch on cream Zweigart 'Linda', 27 threads to 1in (2.5cm).
Finished size – 6×4¾in (15.2×12cm).
Cut fabric to fit an 8in (20cm) embroidery hoop.

TO MOUNT
Follow the mounting instructions (Method 2) on p123.
*You will need:*
☐ White card – 8¼×15in (21×38cm) to make a top-folded card
☐ White backing card – 8¼×7½in (21×19cm)
☐ Window template – 64 squares × 52, cut from graph paper which has 10 squares to 1in (2.5cm)

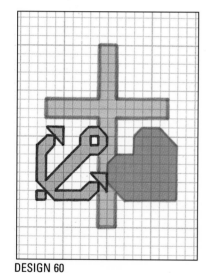

DESIGN 60

### DESIGN 60

| ANCHOR | | DMC |
|---|---|---|
| 0398 | ▧ | 318 |
| 0891 | ▧ | 676 |
| 066 | ▧ | 3688 |

**BACK STITCH**

| | | |
|---|---|---|
| | — | Fil argent |
| 068 | — | 3687 |
| | — | Fil or mi-fin |

### DESIGN 61

| ANCHOR | | DMC |
|---|---|---|
| 0891 | ▧ | 676 |
| 0923 | ▨ | 700 |
| 0310 | ▨ | 434 |
| 013 | ▨ | 349 |
| 0128 | ▧ | 800 |
| 0295 | ▧ | 726 |
| 0386 | ▧ | 746 |
| 01 | ☐ | blanc |
| 0403 | ■ | 310 |

**BACK STITCH**

| | | |
|---|---|---|
| 0403 | — | 310 |
| 0923 | — | 700 |
| 0295 | — | 726 |

**FRENCH KNOTS**

| | | |
|---|---|---|
| 0403 | ● | 310 |

DESIGN 61

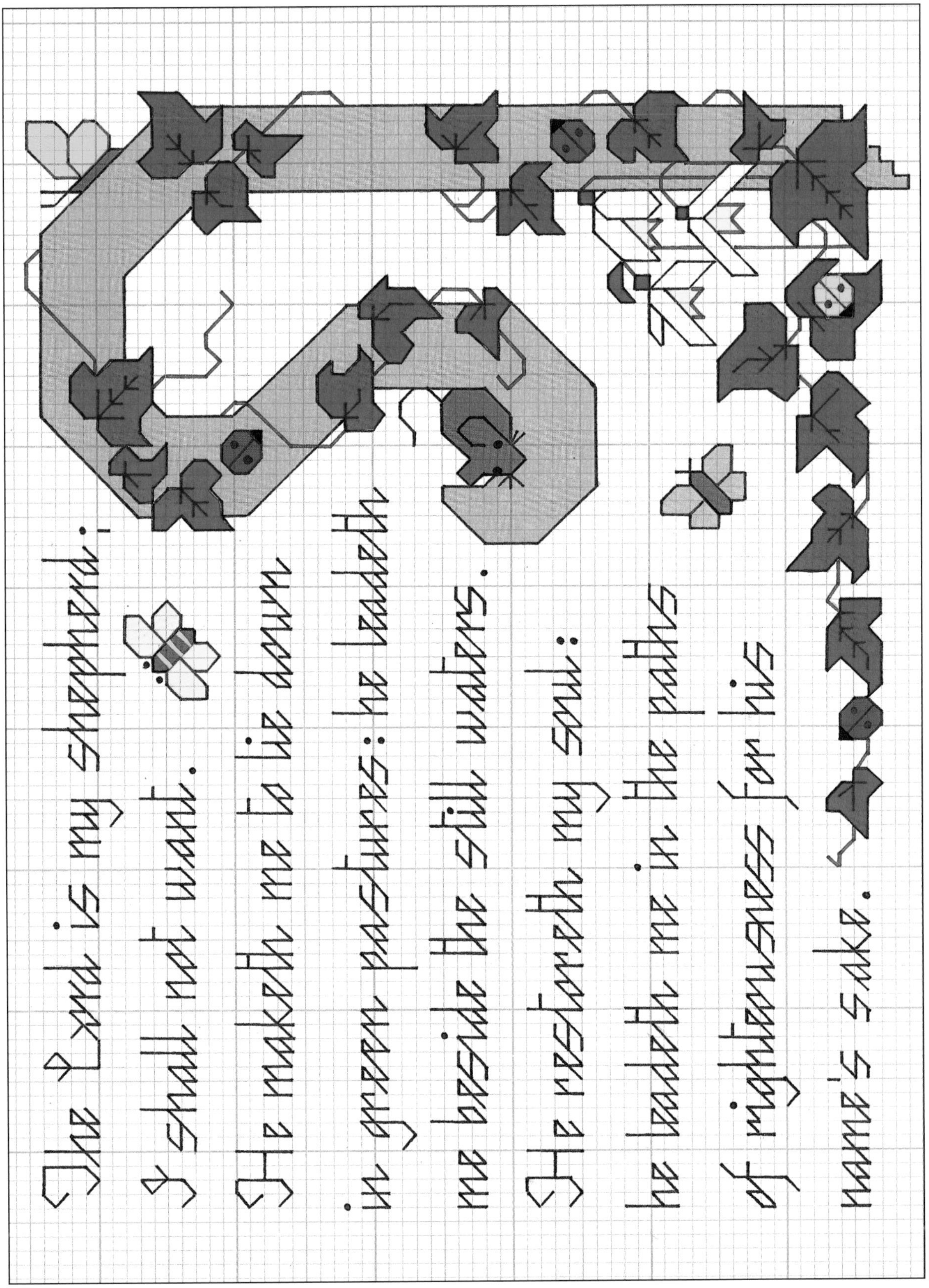

The Lord is my shepherd;

I shall not want.

He maketh me to lie down

in green pastures: he leadeth

me beside the still waters.

He restoreth my soul:

he leadeth me in the paths

of righteousness for his

name's sake.

# *Festivals Worldwide*

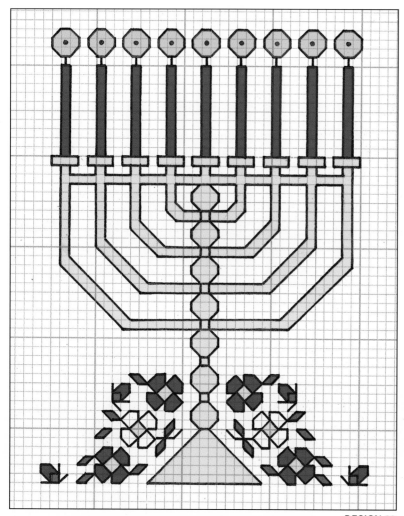

DESIGN 62

| DESIGN 62 | | |
|---|---|---|
| ANCHOR | | DMC |
| 0907 | □ | 833 |
| 0229 | ■ | 910 |
| 09046 | ■ | 321 |
| 01 | □ | blanc |
| **GOLD SEQUINS** | | |
| | ▫ | |
| **BACK STITCH** | | |
| 0403 | – | 310 |

| DESIGN 63 | | |
|---|---|---|
| ANCHOR | | DMC |
| 01 | □ | blanc |
| 09046 | ■ | 321 |
| 0228 | ■ | 701 |
| 0305 | □ | 743 |
| 077 | ■ | 602 |
| 0100 | ■ | 552 |
| 0137 | ■ | 792 |
| **BACK STITCH** | | |
| 0403 | – | 310 |
| **FRENCH KNOTS** | | |
| 0305 | ● | 743 |

# CHANUKKAH

The Jewish Festival of Light lasts for eight days. An eight-branched candlestick is placed in the window and on the first evening of Chanukkah one candle is lit, on the second, two, and so on until all eight are lit on the final evening. The ninth candle is the servant candle which is used to light all the others.

Stitch on cream Zweigart 'Linda', 27 threads to 1in (2.5cm).
Finished size – 2¾×3¾in (7× 9.5cm).

Cut fabric to fit a 5in (13cm) embroidery hoop.
For each candle flame, sew on a gold sequin held in place with a tiny yellow bead (Fig 34a).

TO MOUNT
Follow the mounting instructions (Method 2) on p123.
*You will need:*
□ Gold card – 11×7in (28× 17.8cm) to make a side-folded card
□ White backing card – 5½× 7in (14×17.8cm)
□ Window template – 35 squares × 45, cut from graph paper which has 10 squares to 1in (2.5cm)

# ROSH HASHANAH

A floral Star of David marks the Jewish New Year.

Stitch on cream Zweigart 'Linda', 27 threads to 1in (2.5cm).
Finished size – 4¾in (12cm) diameter circle.
Cut fabric to fit a 6in (15cm) embroidery hoop.

## TO MOUNT
Follow the mounting instructions (Method 2) on p123.

*You will need:*
☐ Red card – 14×8in (35.6×20.3cm) to make a side-folded card
☐ White backing card – 7×8in (17.8×20.3cm)

For the window cut a 5in (12.7cm) diameter circle, using a compass cutter. Trim the card with a small bunch of artificial flowers. Gather the flowers into a bunch, tie together with a bow of 1.5mm green ribbon and glue to the card to provide a finishing touch.

**DESIGN 63**

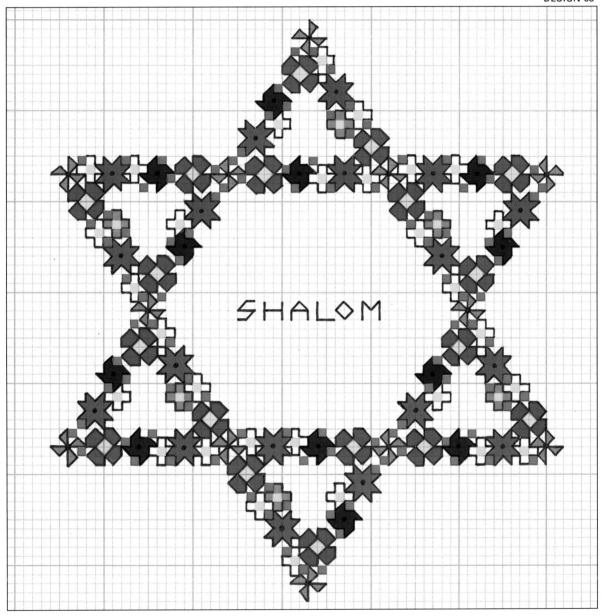

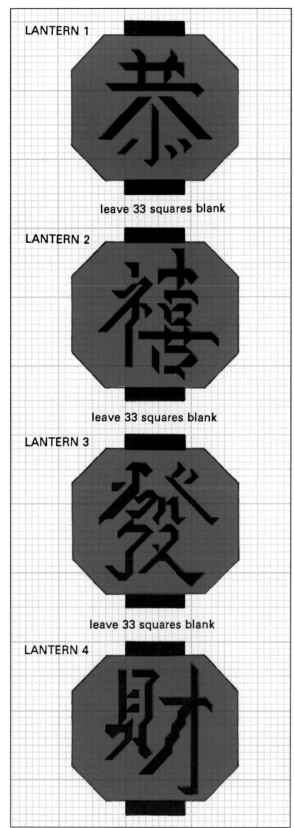

LANTERN 1

leave 33 squares blank

LANTERN 2

leave 33 squares blank

LANTERN 3

leave 33 squares blank

LANTERN 4

DESIGN 64

# CHINESE NEW YEAR

Make a wall hanging which wishes a happy and prosperous New Year. The words are written on Chinese lanterns which decorate homes and streets at this time of year.

Stitch on cream deluxe Hardanger, Zweigart 'Oslo', 22 blocks to 1in (2.5cm).
Finished size of each lantern – 2¼×2¼in (5.7× 5.7cm).
Cut fabric 9×26in (23×66cm).
Stitch the top of the first lantern centrally 3in (7.6cm) from the top of the fabric. Leave a space of 33 squares on the chart between the lanterns to allow room for the tassels which are added later.

TO MAKE UP
Follow the instructions given on p20.
*You will need:*
☐ 4×2½in (6.3cm) tassels made from DMC Fil or mi-fin (Fig 45)
☐ 1 pair × 4in (10cm) brass hangers
☐ White sewing thread

When the hanging is mounted, sew on a tassel under each lantern.

# ID UL-FITR

The family festival of Islam, celebrated at the end of Ramadan. This adaptation of an Islamic tile pattern has been mounted as a needle case, but also can be used to make a very effective card.

Stitch on dark blue 'Aida', 14 blocks to 1in (2.5cm).
Finished size – 3¾×3¾in (9.5×9.5cm).
Cut fabric 10½×5in (26.7×12.7cm).

TO MAKE UP
Allowing ½in (1.5cm) for turnings, turn all raw edges to the wrong side of the fabric and stick down using a thin coat of glue. Mitre each corner so that it lies flat (Fig 10a). With pinking shears, cut a piece of felt 9¼×4in (23.5×10.2cm). Glue the felt to the inside of the needlecase, so that it covers the raw edges of the 'Aida'. Add a press fastener to the side edges (Fig 10b). On the outside of the needlecase sew a decorative button over the press fastener. Lastly, fill the needlecase with needles.

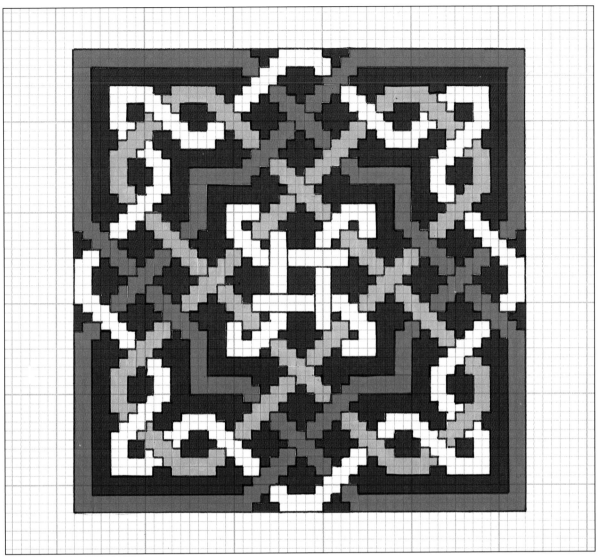

DESIGN 65

½in (1.5cm) turning allowance

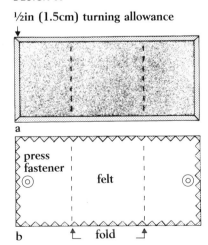

a

press
fastener

felt

b    fold

**Fig 10** *Making up a needlecase*

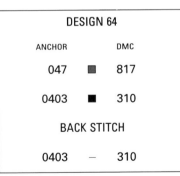

| DESIGN 64 | | |
|---|---|---|
| ANCHOR | | DMC |
| 047 | ■ | 817 |
| 0403 | ■ | 310 |
| **BACK STITCH** | | |
| 0403 | – | 310 |

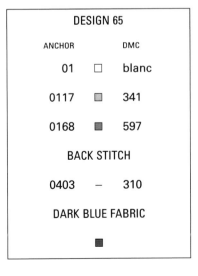

| DESIGN 65 | | |
|---|---|---|
| ANCHOR | | DMC |
| 01 | □ | blanc |
| 0117 | ▨ | 341 |
| 0168 | ▥ | 597 |
| **BACK STITCH** | | |
| 0403 | – | 310 |
| **DARK BLUE FABRIC** | | |
| | ■ | |

DESIGN 66

| DESIGN 66 | | |
|-----------|---|---|
| ANCHOR | | DMC |
| 0112 | ■ | 208 |
| 0133 | ■ | 796 |
| 0306 | □ | 725 |
| 0230 | ■ | 909 |
| BACK STITCH | | |
| 0403 | − | 310 |
| | − | Fil or mi-fin |
| FRENCH KNOTS | | |
| | ● | Fil or mi-fin |

| DESIGN 67 | | |
|-----------|---|---|
| ANCHOR | | DMC |
| 022 | ■ | 815 |
| 0330 | ■ | 946 |
| 0403 | ■ | 310 |
| 0134 | ■ | 820 |
| 0102 | ■ | 550 |
| 0923 | ■ | 699 |
| 085 | ■ | 3609 |
| 088 | ■ | 718 |
| 0298 | □ | 972 |
| BACK STITCH - Optional | | |
| 0403 | − | 310 |

# DIWALI

The Hindu Festival of Light is a time of great celebration when houses are illuminated traditionally with clay lamps.

Stitch on red Zweigart 'Linda', 27 threads to 1in (2.5cm). Finished size – 2¾×3½in (7× 8.9cm). Cut fabric to fit a 5in (13cm) embroidery hoop. For extra glitter, when the embroidery is finished, add some small star-shaped sequins and gold beads (Fig 34a) to the spaces between the lamps.

TO MOUNT
Follow the mounting instructions (Method 2) on p123.
*You will need:*
☐ Dark blue card – 10½×6½in (26.6×16.5cm) to make a side-folded card
☐ Dark blue backing card – 5¼×6½in (13.3×16.5cm)
☐ Window template – use Template 4 on p118, traced onto thin card

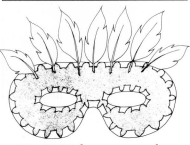

**Fig 11** *Making up a mask*

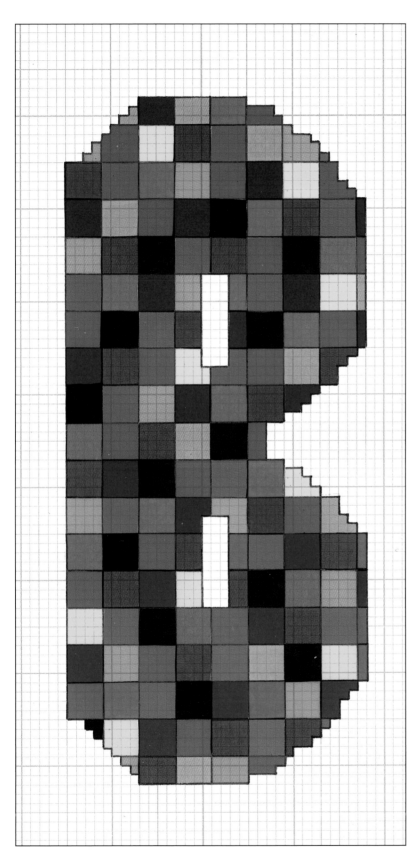

# MARDI GRAS

On this day of flamboyant carnival celebration before the forty-day fast of Lent begins, exotic and colourful masks are worn in street processions.

Stitch on red or dark blue 'Aida', 11 blocks to 1in (2.5cm). Finished size – 6½×3in (16.5× 7.6cm).
Cut fabric to fit an 8in (20cm) embroidery hoop.

TO MAKE UP
Cut one thick card mask using Template 5 on p117. Stick the embroidery to this using a thin application of glue. Trim away all excess fabric to within ½in (1.5cm) of the mask. Clip all curves and glue the excess fabric to the back of the mask. Slit the embroidery with care centrally along the length of the eye holes. Turn the raw edges to the back and glue them down. Glue a row of coloured feathers along the top of the mask (Fig 11). Cut another mask from black felt and glue this over the back to hide all the raw edges of the 'Aida' and the ends of the feathers. Cover a knitting needle by glueing coloured ribbons in a spiral fashion along its length. Fix the knitting needle with glue to the back of the mask on one side to form a handle. Trim the handle by knotting around it ½yd (50cm) each of Offray Black (030), Emerald (580), Torrid Orange (750), Wine (275), Rosewood (169), Bright Yellow (657), Rose Pink (154) and Mulberry (475) 3mm ribbon. Sew some brightly coloured sequins and beads to the ends of the ribbons.
You are now fully equipped to go out and paint the town red in complete anonymity.

DESIGN 67

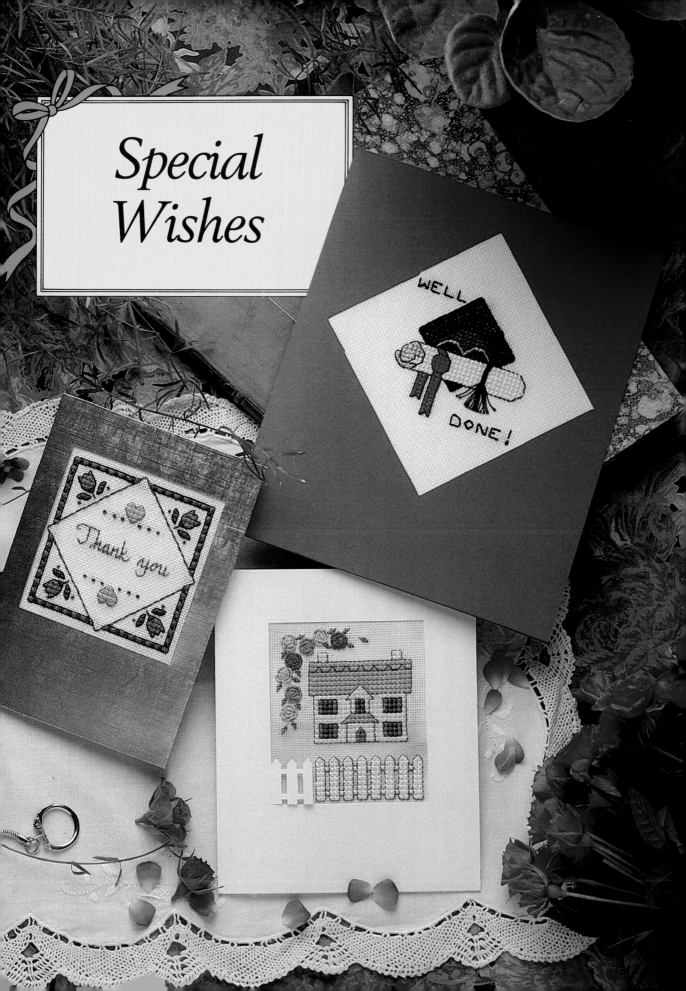

# Special Wishes

# THANK YOU

Stitch on cream deluxe Hardanger, Zweigart 'Oslo', 22 blocks to 1in (2.5cm).
Finished size – 3×3in (7.6×7.6cm).
Cut fabric to fit a 5in (13cm) embroidery hoop.
As an alternative to black, the lettering can be stitched using dark purple thread, 208 (0111).

TO MOUNT
Follow the mounting instructions (Method 1) on p122.
*You will need:*
☐ 1 silver ready-made card mount with a window 3¼×3¼in (8.2×8.2cm)

DESIGN 68

| DESIGN 68 | | | | |
|---|---|---|---|---|
| ANCHOR | DMC | ANCHOR | | DMC |
| 0212 ■ | 991 | BACK STITCH | | |
| 0108 ■ | 210 | 0403 | – | 310 |
| 0111 ■ | 208 | 0212 | – | 991 |
| 0133 ■ | 796 | FRENCH KNOTS | | |
| | | 0212 ● | | 991 |
| | | 0301 ● | | 744 |

# GOOD LUCK

Stitch on cream deluxe Hardanger, Zweigart 'Oslo', 22 blocks to 1in (2.5cm).
Finished size – 3¼×4¼in (8.2×10.8cm).
Cut fabric to fit a 6in (15cm) embroidery hoop.
To work the border you will need 1yd (1m) Berisfords Yellow (37) 3mm ribbon. Couch the ribbon to the surface of the fabric using cross stitches (Fig 4), at the positions indicated on the chart. Tie the two loose ends of ribbon in a bow at the top left-hand corner and

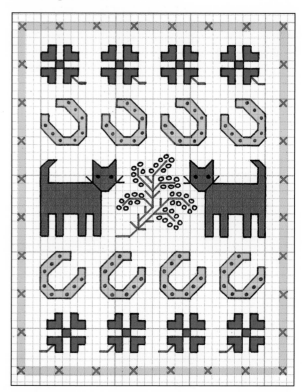

DESIGN 69

| DESIGN 69 | | | | |
|---|---|---|---|---|
| ANCHOR | DMC | ANCHOR | | DMC |
| 0229 ■ | 701 | FRENCH KNOTS | | |
| 0400 ■ | 413 | 0403 ● | | 310 |
| 0306 ☐ | 725 | 01 ○ | | blanc |
| BACK STITCH | | COUCHING STITCHES | | |
| 0403 – | 310 | 0229 × | | 701 |
| 0229 – | 701 | | | |

trim the ends to length when the card is finished.

## TO MOUNT
Follow the mounting instructions (Method 1) on p122.
*You will need:*
☐ 1 ready-made cream card with a window 3¾×5½in (9.5× 14cm)

To trim, stick two gold horse shoes (cake decorations) to the finished card, positioning them diagonally opposite the bow of ribbon.

DESIGN 70

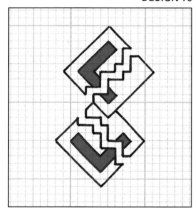

# DRIVING TEST SUCCESS

This is a real 'quickie'.

Stitch on cream Zweigart 'Belfast', 30 threads to 1in (2.5cm).
Finished size – ¾×1½in (1.9× 3.8cm).
Cut fabric to fit a 2½in (6cm) embroidery hoop.

## TO MOUNT
*You will need:*
☐ 1 Framecraft 1½×2in (3.8× 5.1cm) oval frame with a key ring attachment

| DESIGN 70 | | |
|---|---|---|
| ANCHOR | | DMC |
| 046 | ■ | 349 |
| 01 | ☐ | blanc |
| BACK STITCH | | |
| 0403 | – | 310 |

Follow the manufacturer's instructions to mount your embroidery into the key ring. Alternatively, work the design on 'Oslo' fabric and place it in a small ready-made card mount.

| DESIGN 71 | | |
|---|---|---|
| ANCHOR | | DMC |
| 0403 | ■ | 310 |
| 0401 | ■ | 844 |
| 0900 | ☐ | 648 |
| 046 | ■ | 666 |
| 0386 | ☐ | 746 |
| BACK STITCH | | |
| 0403 | – | 310 |
| FRENCH KNOTS | | |
| 0403 | ● | 310 |

# GRADUATION

Stitch on cream deluxe Hardanger, Zweigart 'Oslo', 22 blocks to 1in (2.5cm).
Finished size – 2¾×2¾in (7×7cm).
Cut fabric to fit a 5in (13cm) embroidery hoop.
When the embroidery is complete, attach 3×6 strands of black stranded cotton to the right-hand edge of the academic cap. Plait the strands for 1in (2.5cm). Make a knot at the end of the plait and trim the ends ¼in (7mm) below the knot. Allow the plait to hang down freely as a tassel.

## TO MOUNT
Follow the mounting instructions (Method 2) on p123.
*You will need:*
☐ Red card – 13×8in (33×20.3cm) to make a side-folding card
☐ White backing card – 6½×8in (16.5×20.3cm)
☐ Window template – 39 squares × 39, cut from graph paper which has 10 squares to 1in (2.5cm)

DESIGN 71

Place the template at a 45° angle to the card to cut a diamond-shaped window.

# GET WELL SOON

Stitch on cream deluxe Hardanger, Zweigart
'Oslo', 22 blocks to 1in (2.5cm).
Finished size – 1¾×3¾in (4.4×9.5cm).
Cut fabric to fit a 5in (13cm) embroidery hoop.

TO MOUNT
Follow the mounting instructions (Method 1) on
p122.
*You will need:*
☐ 1 white ready-made card mount with a window
2¾×4¼in (7×10.8cm)

| DESIGN 72 | | | | | |
|---|---|---|---|---|---|
| ANCHOR | | DMC | ANCHOR | | DMC |
| 077 | ■ | 602 | 0229 | ■ | 701 |
| 0137 | ■ | 792 | 0303 | ■ | 741 |
| 01 | ☐ | blanc | BACK STITCH | | |
| 0305 | ■ | 743 | 0403 | – | 310 |

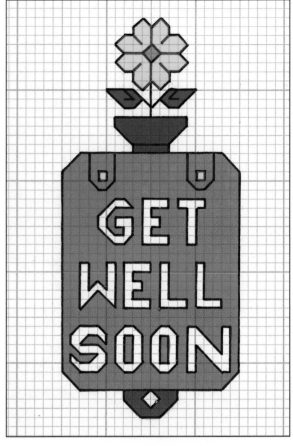

DESIGN 72

# MEDICINE TRAY

Carry cups of tea or medicine to the sickroom on
this tray which also offers a word of
encouragement for the patient.

Stitch on cream deluxe Hardanger, Zweigart
'Oslo', 22 blocks to 1in (2.5cm).
Finished size – 4½×2½in (11.4×6.3cm).
Cut fabric 11½×11½in (29×29cm).
Embroider the bottom right-hand corner of the
medicine bottle 2in (5cm) up from the bottom of
the fabric and 2in (5cm) in from the right-hand
side of the fabric. To speed things along, the glass
of the thermometer, beaker and bottle top can be
left as bare fabric outlined in back stitch.
Mount according to the manufacturer's
instructions in a Framecraft small, square, wooden
tray, measuring 9½×9½in (24×24cm).

DESIGN 73

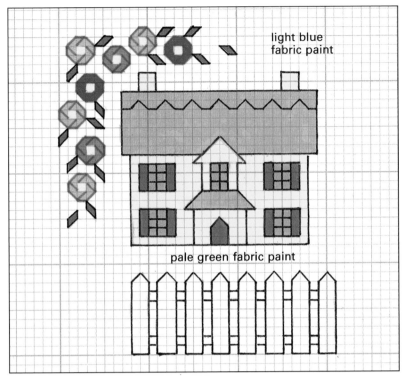

light blue
fabric paint

pale green fabric paint

DESIGN 74

# WELCOME TO YOUR NEW HOME

Stitch on cream deluxe Hardanger, Zweigart 'Oslo', 22 blocks to 1in (2.5cm).

| DESIGN 73 | | |
|---|---|---|
| ANCHOR | | DMC |
| 01 | ☐ | blanc |
| 063 | ▨ | 602 |
| 0132 | ▧ | 797 |
| 09046 | ■ | 321 |
| 0230 | ■ | 909 |
| 0297 | ▨ | 726 |
| BACK STITCH | | |
| 0403 | – | 310 |

Finished size – 2¾×3¼in (7× 8.2cm).
Cut fabric to fit a 5in (13cm) embroidery hoop.
Before stitching, paint the fabric as indicated on the chart, following the instructions on p119. The roses can be cross stitched, or can be worked as bullion bars (Fig 31b).

TO MOUNT
Follow the mounting instructions (Method 2) on p123.
*You will need:*
☐ White card – 10×6in (25.4× 15.2cm) to make a side-folded card
☐ White backing card – 5×6in (12.7×15.2cm)
☐ Window template – use Template 6 on p118 traced onto thin card

Cut out the window, leaving the gate attached to the card. Score the left-hand side of the gate so that it can be bent open.

| DESIGN 74 | | |
|---|---|---|
| ANCHOR | | DMC |
| 0387 | ☐ | écru |
| 08581 | ▨ | 647 |
| 0215 | ■ | 320 |
| 0943 | ▨ | 422 |
| 073 | ▨ | 3689 |
| 066 | ▨ | 3688 |
| 068 | ■ | 3687 |
| 01 | ☐ | blanc |
| BACK STITCH | | |
| 0401 | – | 844 |
| 068 | – | 3687 |

# BASKET PINCUSHION

This tiny gift (see p100) can be given on any occasion and takes very little time to make. Your choice of fabric and dimensions will depend on the size of the basket you choose. Embroider one of the flower motifs from the Christening Rattle (p86) on a small circle of fabric, then sew a running thread around the edge of the circle. Make a ball with some Fibrefill stuffing and gather the fabric circle around the ball by pulling up the running thread to form a small cushion. Insert the cushion into a miniature basket and glue into place. Trim with fabric flowers and ribbon.

# FRIENDSHIP

An Arabian proverb; stitch on Zweigart 'Belfast', 30 threads to 1in (2.5cm).
Finished size – 3½×4½in (8.9×11.4cm).
Cut fabric to fit a 6in (15cm) embroidery hoop.

TO MOUNT
Follow the mounting instructions (Method 2) on p123.

*You will need:*
☐ White card covered with pale orange tissue paper – 12×7¼in (31×18.4cm) to make a side-folded card
☐ White backing card – 6×7¼in (15.5×18.4cm)
☐ Window template – 40 squares × 53, cut from graph paper which has 10 squares to 1in (2.5cm)

| DESIGN 75 | | |
|---|---|---|
| ANCHOR | | DMC |
| 046 | ■ | 666 |
| 0253 | ▢ | 472 |
| 0238 | ■ | 704 |
| 0227 | ■ | 702 |
| 0175 | ▢ | 794 |
| 0309 | ■ | 976 |
| 0891 | ▢ | 676 |
| 0901 | ■ | 680 |
| BACK STITCH | | |
| 0400 | — | 317 |
| 0227 | — | 702 |
| FRENCH KNOTS | | |
| 0400 | ● | 317 |

A friend is one
To whom one may pour
Out all the contents
Of one's heart,
Chaff and grain together
Knowing that the
Gentlest of hands
Will take and sift it,
Keeping what is worth keeping
And with a breath of kindness
Blow the rest away....

DESIGN 75

A friend is one
To whom one may pour
Out all the contents
Of one's heart
Chaff and grain together,
Knowing that the
Gentlest of hands
Will take and sift it,
Keeping what is worth keeping
And with a breath of kindness
Blow the rest away...

# MINIATURE GARDEN

This card would be especially suitable to celebrate a retirement or as a gift for a keen gardener.

Stitch on cream deluxe Hardanger, Zweigart 'Oslo', 22 blocks to 1in (2.5cm).
Finished size – 3½×4¾in (9×12cm).
Cut fabric to fit a 7in (18cm) embroidery hoop.
The lettuces and cauliflowers can be worked as

bullion bars (Fig 31b).

TO MOUNT
Follow the mounting instructions (Method 2) p123.
*You will need:*
☐ White card covered with green, mottled paper – 12×7¼in (31×18.4cm) to make a side-folded card
☐ White backing card – 6×7¼in (15.5×18.4cm)
☐ Window template – 40 squares × 53, cut from graph paper which has 10 squares to 1in (2.5cm)

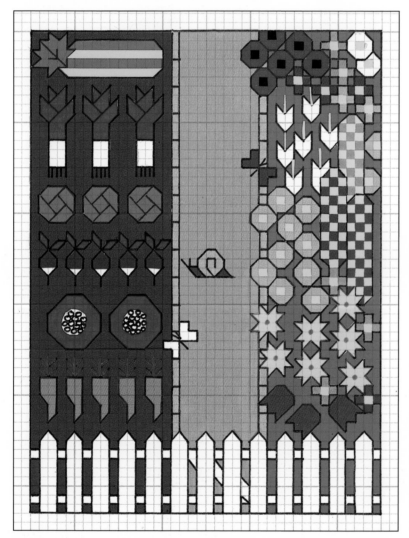

DESIGN 76

| DESIGN 76 | | |
|---|---|---|
| ANCHOR | | DMC |
| 0403 | ■ | 310 |
| 09046 | ■ | 321 |
| 0799 | ■ | 498 |
| 0130 | ■ | 799 |
| 0295 | ▢ | 726 |
| 0887 | ▢ | 3046 |
| 0357 | ■ | 975 |
| 0231 | ▢ | 453 |
| 0330 | ■ | 946 |
| 0109 | ▢ | 209 |
| 075 | ▢ | 3326 |
| 0226 | ■ | 702 |
| 0923 | ■ | 699 |
| 01 | ☐ | blanc |
| **BACK STITCH** | | |
| 0403 | — | 310 |
| 0295 | ⋯ | 726 |
| 0226 | – | 702 |
| **FRENCH KNOTS** | | |
| 01 | ○ | blanc |
| 0330 | ● | 946 |

108

# The Final Curtain

sky - light blue fabric paint

field - light brown fabric paint

field - brown fabric paint

# SPRING HAS SPRUNG

Stitch on cream Zweigart 'Linda', 27 threads to 1in (2.5cm).
Finished size – 4½×3¼in (11.4×8.2cm). Cut fabric to fit a 7in (18cm) embroidery hoop.
Before stitching, paint the fabric as indicated on the chart, following the instructions on p119.
The hyacinths can be worked in French knots.

### TO MOUNT
Follow the mounting instructions (Method 2) on p123.
*You will need:*
☐ White card covered with mini-print paper – 9× 14in (23×35.6cm) to make a top-folded card
☐ White backing card – 9×7in (23×17.8cm)
☐ Window template – 46 squares × 32, cut from graph paper which has 10 squares to 1in (2.5cm)

### TO TRIM
*You will need:*
☐ White card covered with mini-print paper (pelmet) – 7½×¾in (19×2cm)
☐ Scraps of cotton-print fabric and ribbon for curtains and tie-backs
☐ UHU glue

| DESIGN 77 | | | | | |
|---|---|---|---|---|---|
| ANCHOR | | DMC | ANCHOR | | DMC |
| 0358 | ■ | 433 | 0301 | ▣ | 744 |
| 0227 | ■ | 702 | 01 | ☐ | blanc |
| 060 | ■ | 604 | 01 | ⊡ | blanc |
| 0160 | ▣ | 519 | **FRENCH KNOTS** | | |
| 0852 | ▢ | 3047 | 0403 | ● | 310 |
| 0943 | ▢ | 3045 | **BACK STITCH** | | |
| 0400 | ■ | 645 | 0403 | – | 310 |
| 0403 | ■ | 310 | 0227 | – | 702 |

Make curtains from strips of cotton-print fabric, turning the side and bottom raw edges to the back and glueing them out of sight. Gather the curtains at the top with a few folds and glue the tops of the curtains either side of the window and slightly above it. Glue the card pelmet over the tops of the curtains above the window to hide all raw edges. Tie a bow of ribbon around each curtain to look like a tie-back.

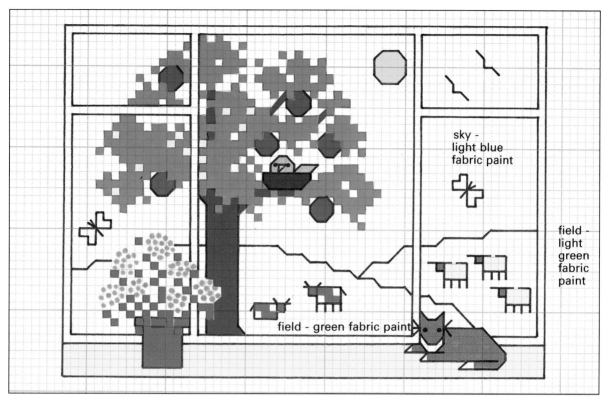

# HIGH SUMMER

Stitch on cream Zweigart 'Linda', 27 threads to
1in (2.5cm).
Finished size – 4½×3¼in (11.4×8.2cm).
Cut fabric to fit a 7in (18cm) embroidery hoop.
Before stitching, paint the fabric as indicated on
the chart, following the instructions on p119.

TO MOUNT
Follow the mounting instructions (Method 2) on
p123.
*You will need:*
☐ White card covered with mini-print paper – 9×
14in (23×35.6cm) to make a top-folded card
☐ White backing card – 9×7in (23×17.8cm)
☐ Window template – 46 squares × 32, cut from
graph paper which has 10 squares to 1in (2.5cm)

TO TRIM
*You will need:*
☐ White card covered with mini-print paper
(pelmet) – 7½×¾in (19×2cm)
☐ Scraps of lace and ribbon for curtains, blind and
tie-backs
☐ UHU glue

Glue a narrow length of lace along the top of the

| DESIGN 78 | | | | |
|---|---|---|---|---|
| ANCHOR | | DMC | ANCHOR | DMC |
| 01 | ☐ | blanc | 0400 ■ | 645 |
| 0227 | ■ | 702 | 0852 ☐ | 3047 |
| 0230 | ■ | 700 | 0301 ☐ | 744 |
| 0358 | ■ | 433 | FRENCH KNOTS | |
| 0381 | ■ | 838 | 0400 ● | 645 |
| 047 | ■ | 817 | 060 ● | 604 |
| 0349 | ■ | 301 | BACK STITCH | |
| 0943 | ☐ | 3045 | 0400 – | 645 |

window to look like a blind. Make curtains from
strips of lace, turning the side and bottom raw
edges to the back and glueing them out of sight.
Gather the curtains at the top with a few folds
and glue the tops of the curtains either side of the
window and slightly above it. Glue the card
pelmet over the tops of the curtains above the
window to hide all raw edges. Tie a bow of ribbon
around each curtain to look like a tie-back.

111

# AUTUMN SUNSET

Stitch on cream Zweigart 'Linda', 27 threads to
1in (2.5cm).
Finished size – 4½×3¼in (11.4×8.2cm).
Cut fabric to fit a 7in (18cm) embroidery hoop.
Before stitching, paint the fabric as indicated on
the chart, following the instructions on p119.

## TO MOUNT
Follow the mounting instructions (Method 2) on
p123.
*You will need:*
☐ White card covered with mini-print paper – 9×
14in (23×35.6cm) to make a top-folded card
☐ White backing card – 9×7in (23×17.8cm)
☐ Window template – 46 squares × 32, cut from
graph paper which has 10 squares to 1in (2.5cm)

## TO TRIM
*You will need:*
☐ White card covered with mini-print paper
(pelmet) – 7½×¾in (19×2cm)
☐ Scraps of cotton-print fabric and ribbon for
curtains and tie-backs
☐ UHU glue

Make curtains from strips of cotton-print fabric,

| DESIGN 79 | | | | |
|---|---|---|---|---|
| ANCHOR | DMC | | ANCHOR | DMC |
| 0227 ■ | 702 | | 0301 □ | 744 |
| 01 □ | blanc | | 0852 □ | 3047 |
| 0381 ■ | 838 | | FRENCH KNOTS | |
| 0358 ■ | 433 | | 0403 ● | 310 |
| 0309 ■ | 976 | | BACK STITCH | |
| 0943 ▨ | 3045 | | 0403 – | 310 |
| 0332 ■ | 900 | | CROSS STITCH over 1 thread | |
| 047 ■ | 817 | | 047 × | 817 |
| 0119 ■ | 333 | | | |

turning the side and bottom raw edges to the back
and glueing them out of sight. Gather at the top
with a few folds and glue the tops either side of
the window and slightly above it. Glue the card
pelmet over the tops of the curtains above the
window and hide all raw edges. Tie a bow of
ribbon around each curtain to look like a tie-back.

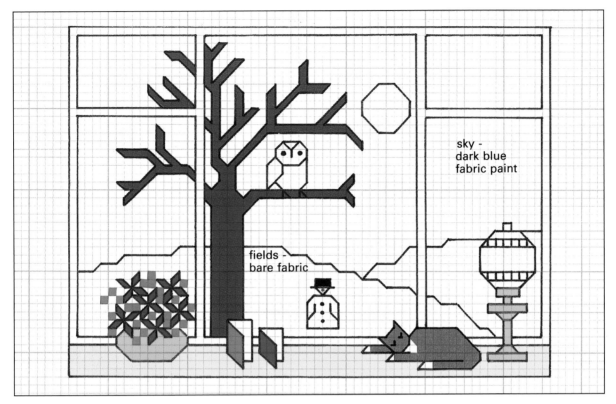

# WINTER SNOW SCENE

Stitch on cream Zweigart 'Linda', 27 threads to 1in (2.5cm).
Finished size – 4½×3¼in (11.4×8.2cm).
Cut fabric to fit a 7in (18cm) embroidery hoop.
Before stitching, paint the fabric as indicated on the chart, following the instructions on p119.

## TO MOUNT
Follow the mounting instructions (Method 2) on p123.
*You will need:*
☐ White card covered with mini-print paper – 9× 14in (23×35.6cm) to make a top-folded card
☐ White backing card – 9×7in (23×17.8cm)
☐ Window template – 46 squares × 32, cut from graph paper which has 10 squares to 1in (2.5cm)

## TO TRIM
*You will need:*
☐ White card covered with mini-print paper (pelmet) 7½×¾in (19×2cm)
☐ Scraps of cotton-print fabric and ribbon for curtains and tie-backs
☐ UHU glue

| DESIGN 80 | | | | | |
|---|---|---|---|---|---|
| ANCHOR | | DMC | ANCHOR | | DMC |
| 0358 | ■ | 433 | 01 | ☐ | blanc |
| 0227 | ■ | 702 | FRENCH KNOTS | | |
| 0306 | ☐ | 725 | 0403 | ● | 310 |
| 047 | ■ | 817 | 047 | ● | 817 |
| 0403 | ■ | 310 | BACK STITCH | | |
| 0400 | ■ | 645 | 0403 | – | 310 |
| 0852 | ☐ | 3047 | | | |

Make curtains from strips of cotton-print fabric, turning the side and bottom raw edges to the back and glueing them out of sight. Gather the curtains at the top with a few folds and glue the tops of the curtains either side of the window and slightly above it. Glue the card pelmet over the tops of the curtains above the window to hide all raw edges. Tie a bow of ribbon around each curtain to look like a tie-back.

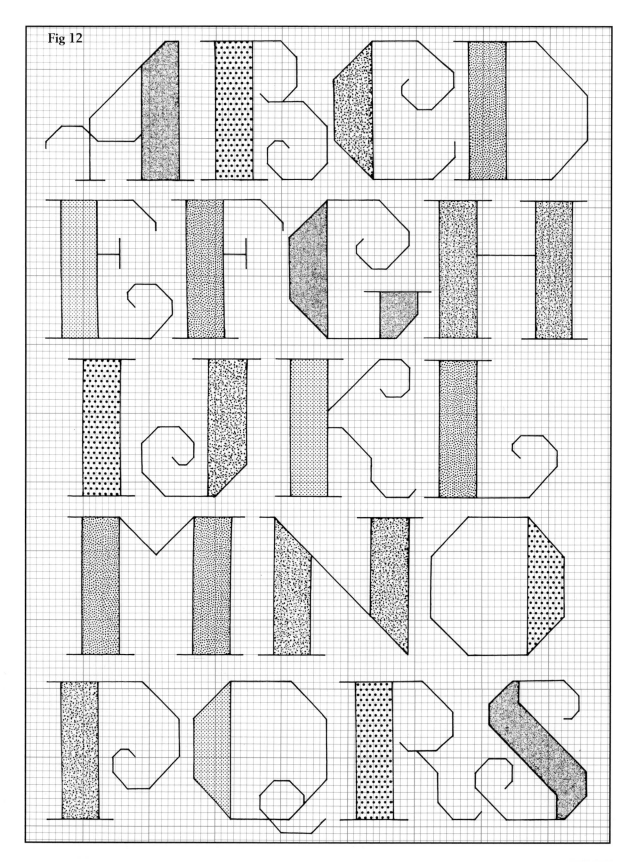

Fig 12

Fig 13

Fig 14

**Fig 15**

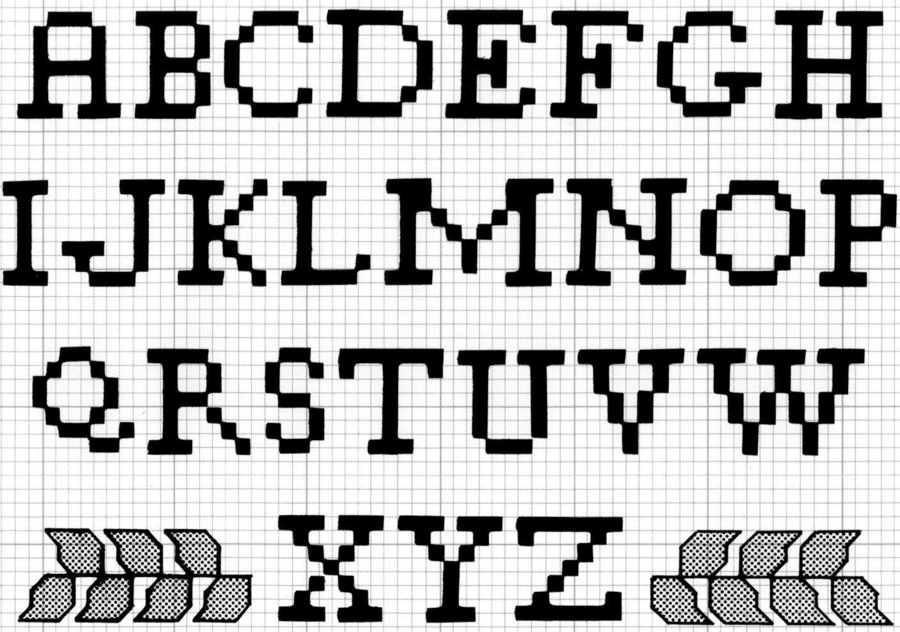

ABCDEFGH
IJKLMNOP
QRSTUVW
XYZ

**Fig 16**

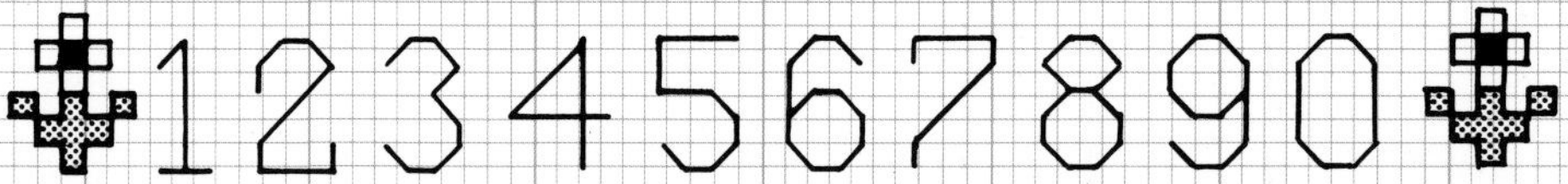

1234567890

**Fig 17**

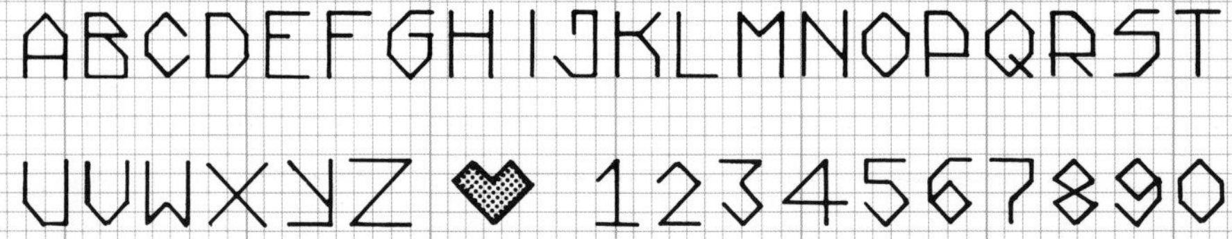

ABCDEFGHIJKLMNOPQRST
UVWXYZ ♥ 1234567890

**Fig 18**

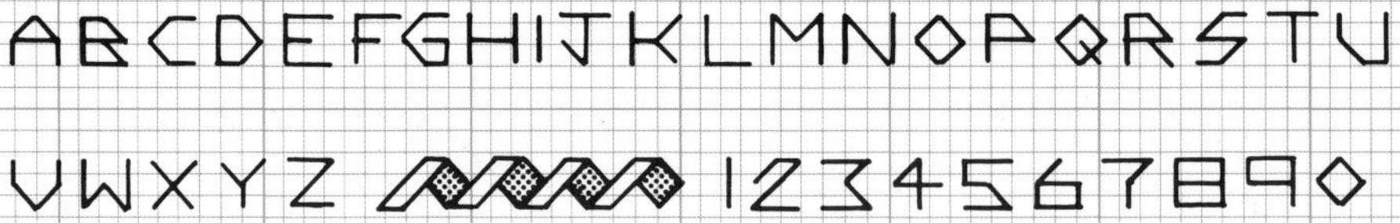

ABCDEFGHIJKLMNOPQRSTU
VWXYZ 1234567890

**Fig 19**

ABCDEFGHIJKLMNOPQRSTUVWXYZ

**Fig 20**

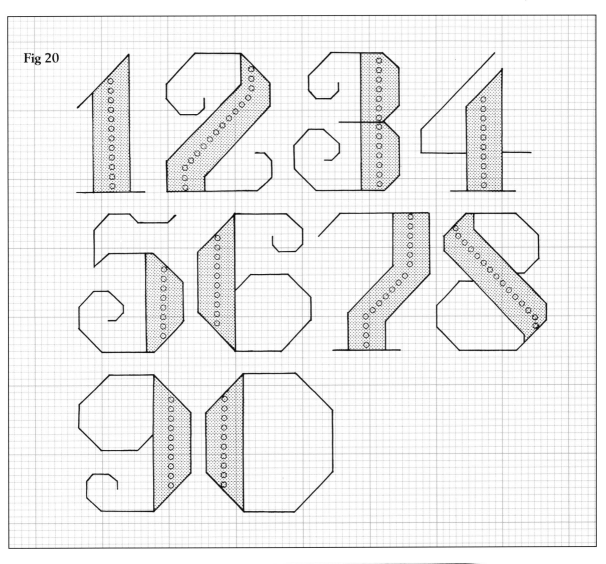

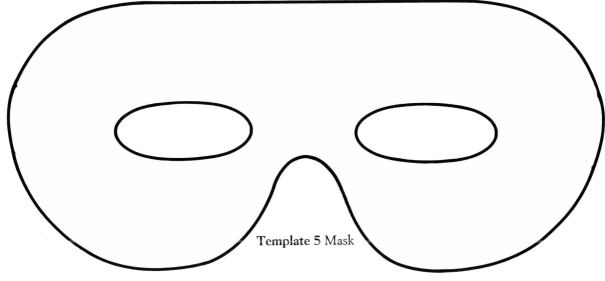

**Template 5** Mask

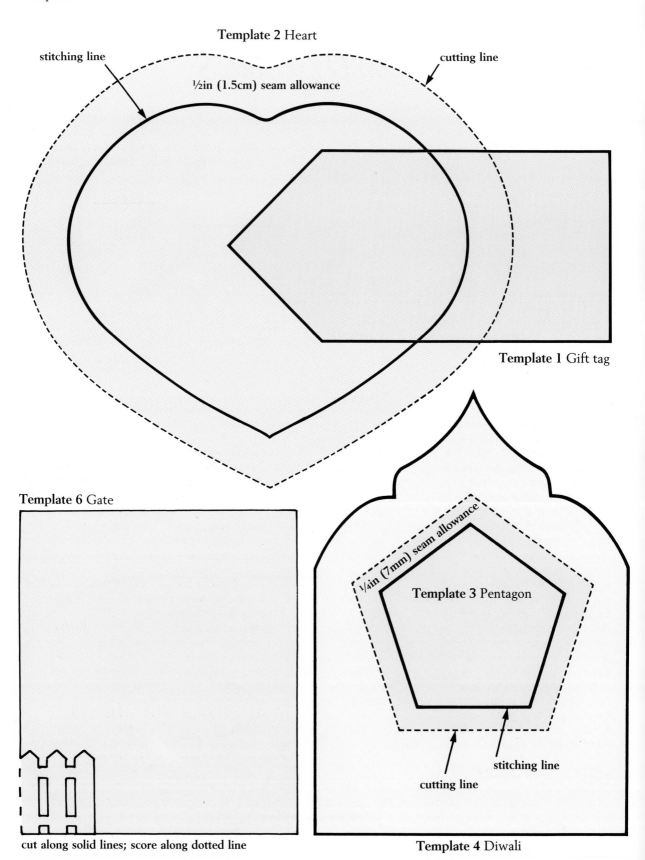

**Template 2** Heart

stitching line

cutting line

½in (1.5cm) seam allowance

**Template 1** Gift tag

**Template 6** Gate

**Template 3** Pentagon

¼in (7mm) seam allowance

stitching line

cutting line

cut along solid lines; score along dotted line

**Template 4** Diwali

# Techniques

## DESIGNING

If the prospect of drawing terrifies you, do not skip this section but read on, for this is drawing made painless.

Before starting to stitch, you might like to add extra design material to the chart. You may wish to add names, dates or other details using the alphabets and numbers provided in this book, or you may want to add extra motifs as in the photograph on p4. In order to do this you will need some graph paper which has 10 squares to 1in (2.5cm). Copy onto a sheet of graph paper (the master sheet) the design that you wish to adapt and put it on one side. On spare graph paper draw out the names, numbers or other material that you wish to incorporate into your design. Cut out each new design element with scissors so that your extra material is on slips of graph paper. Place these slips on the master sheet and move them around until you find a position for them that is pleasing. Try several different layouts for, with this method, you are free to do so without having to erase and re-draw each change. When you are satisfied, glue the slips into position, taking care to line up the squares on the master sheet with the squares on the slips. Your new chart is now ready to stitch.

Study the photograph on p4 and Design 52 and you will see that material has been taken from elsewhere in the book and has been incorporated into the design to make it more personal. The border has been expanded to fit around the larger design. This was achieved by drawing out all the separate elements of the design onto slips of graph paper. Four border strips were drawn out, adding extra pattern repeats to obtain the length required. All the components of the design were then laid on a master sheet and the border strips were placed around them. When a pleasing arrangement had been found, all the slips were glued into position and the new chart was complete. Following these procedures requires no drawing ability and enables you to produce your own designs with ease. For further help and more ambitious designing, consult my first book, *Picture It in Cross Stitch*.

## USING FABRIC PAINT

You do not have to be an artist to use fabric paint. If you see yourself as an embroiderer but not as a Renoir, think of it this way – painting a landscape onto fabric saves you the considerable effort of filling in a landscape with stitching.

First wash your fabric to remove any dressing in it. Allow it to dry thoroughly, iron it to remove all creases and mount it into an embroidery hoop (Fig 21). To give yourself guide lines, following the

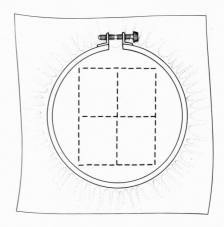

**Fig 21** *Fabric mounted into a hoop*

chart, outline with tacking thread the areas to be painted. Use a fine brush and a fabric paint such as Dylon Color-fun. Experiment on spare scraps of fabric, diluting the paint with water to get softer shades. Paint the fabric as indicated on the chart taking each colour up to the tacked guide lines. Where a clear, precise division is needed between colours it is imperative to keep the brush as dry as possible whilst painting. For a softer effect use lots of water and let the colours 'bleed' into each other. Allow the paint to dry thoroughly and remove the tacking threads before starting to stitch. Following the manufacturer's instructions, iron the fabric to fix the colour. You really cannot go wrong; the blotchier the result the more effective it looks, so do not be put off stitching a design because it calls for fabric paint.

## PREPARING FABRIC FOR STITCHING

Each pattern tells you which fabric to use to get a result similar to the samples in the photographs. The number of threads to 1in (2.5cm) is given so that, if need be, you can substitute another fabric of a similar count.

The finished size given with each pattern refers to the finished size of the embroidered design, not to the finished size of the card or keepsake. If you work on a fabric with a different thread count to that given with the pattern, the finished size will not be the same, and mounting instructions will have to be adapted accordingly.

Cut the fabric so that it will fit into the stated size of embroidery hoop. The fabric should be cut generously, allowing a good 1in (2.5cm) of fabric to overhang the edge of the hoop all round (Fig 21). Oversew the raw edges to stop them fraying. Find the centre of the fabric and mark it temporarily with a pin. Unless instructed otherwise, the centre of the design will be worked at this central point. Mount the fabric into an embroidery hoop, with the central pin lying at the centre of the hoop. With larger designs, cut the fabric to the size stated and work the design in an embroidery frame.

## WORKING STITCHES FROM THE CHART

A full square on the chart indicates the use of a full cross stitch, a right-angled triangle indicates a three-quarter cross stitch, a solid line indicates back stitch and a dot indicates a French knot. Where white thread is to be used in a design it will appear in the colour key, otherwise leave empty squares on the graph as bare fabric; in cross stitch embroidery the background is not worked. Before tackling a project, beginners will need to familiarise themselves with all the required stitches, practising them if necessary on spare fabric until they can be produced with ease.

## WORKING ON DIFFERENT FABRICS
### Zweigart 'Linda' or 'Belfast'
Work over two threads (Fig 22). Use two strands of stranded cotton for cross stitches. Use one strand for back stitches and French knots.

Fig 22 *A full cross stitch worked on 'Linda' or 'Belfast'*

### Deluxe Hardanger, Zweigart 'Oslo'
Work over two blocks (Fig 23). Use three strands of stranded cotton for cross stitches. Use one strand for back stitches and French knots.

Fig 23 *A full cross stitch worked on 'Oslo'*

### 'Aida'
Work over one block (Fig 24).
On 11 count Aida use four strands of stranded cotton for cross stitches.
On 14 count Aida use three strands of stranded cotton for cross stitches.
On 18 count Aida use two strands of stranded cotton for cross stitches.
On all counts, use one strand for back stitches and French knots.
On all fabrics use your discretion when lettering in back stitch.
Sometimes one extra strand will be needed to achieve a less 'spidery' result.

Fig 24 *A full cross stitch worked on 'Aida'*

### Full cross stitch (Fig 25)
When working rows of full cross stitches, bring the needle out at the left-hand side of the row and work a row of half crosses. Return, making the complete crosses, working from right to left and using the same holes as before. All stitches interlock or 'hold hands', sharing holes with their neighbours unless they are single stitches worked on their own.

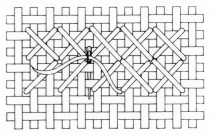

Fig 25 *Working lines of full cross stitches*

## Three-quarter cross stitch (Fig 26)

The first half of the cross stitch is formed in the usual way but the second 'quarter' stitch is brought across and down into the central hole. If working on 'Aida' the 'quarter' stitch must be worked into the centre of the block. Where the chart indicates two three-quarter stitches together, these are worked sharing the same central hole and occupying the space of one full cross stitch (Fig 27).

**Fig 26** *Four examples of three-quarter cross stitches*

**Fig 27** *Two three-quarter cross stitches sewn back to back, occupying the space of one full cross stitch*

## Back stitch (Fig 28)

Most of the designs are finished with a back stitch outline to give definition and detail. As a general rule, outline a pale colour with a darker tone of the same colour if you have it. The colour key will give you the minimum number of colours required for outlining, but do use your discretion, and experiment. Back stitch is worked around and sometimes over the completed cross stitch. It is also used for lettering. Bring the needle out at 1 and in again at 2. Bring it out again at 3 and in again at 4. Continue this sequence in the direction indicated by the chart.

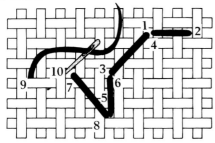

**Fig 28** *Back stitch*

## French knots (Fig 29)

Bring the needle out one thread to the right of where you want the knot to lie. Depending on the size of the knot you require, slip the needle once or twice under the thread so that the twists lie snugly around the needle. Without allowing the thread to untwist, insert the needle back in the fabric one thread to the left of where you started and pull the thread through to the back. For larger knots use more strands of thread or a thicker needle.

**Fig 29** *Working a French knot*

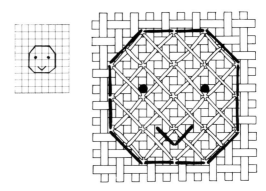

**Fig 30** *Full cross stitch, three-quarter cross stitch, back stitch and French knots combined to stitch a face*

## Bullion bars (Fig 31a)

Bring the needle out at A and, leaving a long loop of thread, reinsert the needle at B, which will determine the length of the bar. Bring the needle out again at A. Wrap the loop of thread six or more times around the needle depending on the length of the bar. Pull the needle through the twists, holding them carefully and stroking them down in the direction A to B. To finish, reinsert your needle at B again. Bullion bars worked in a circle make a pleasing textural alternative to cross stitch when embroidering small roses and brassicas (Fig 31b).

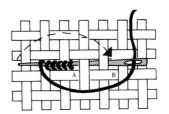

*b) A rose worked in bullion bars*

**Fig 31** *a) Working a bullion bar*

## Stitching Hints

☐ For best results, the full cross stitches should be worked with all the top stitches lying in the same direction.

☐ When starting and finishing a thread, avoid using knots. Loose ends should be sewn into the back of the work.

☐ Do not carry a thread across the back of bare fabric. A trail will show when the work is mounted.

☐ Count the stitches very carefully and frequently check your work against the chart to avoid the frustration of unpicking.

## ADDING BEADS AND SEQUINS

Beads can be incorporated into the embroidery by threading them onto the cross stitches as they are worked. Bring the needle out to make the first half of the cross stitch and thread on a bead. Put the needle into the fabric and pull the thread to the back (Fig 32a). As you make the second half of the cross stitch, thread the needle through the bead again, in the opposite direction (Fig 32b). Beads can be applied directly to the surface of the fabric so that they sit upright (Fig 33a) or so that they lie flat (Fig 33b). Sequins can be sewn on and held in place with beads (Fig 34a), or can be pinned to pillows with pins threaded with beads (Fig 34b).

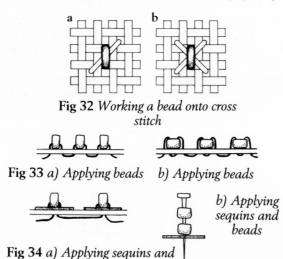

**Fig 32** *Working a bead onto cross stitch*

**Fig 33** *a) Applying beads*   *b) Applying beads*

**Fig 34** *a) Applying sequins and beads*

*b) Applying sequins and beads*

## PRESSING YOUR EMBROIDERY

When all the stitching is complete, press your embroidery to remove any creases. To avoid flattening the stitches lay a white terry towel on a flat surface and place your work face down on the towel. Then cover the work with a thin cloth and press gently with a warm iron.

## MOUNTING EMBROIDERY INTO A CARD
### Method 1: Using ready-made mounts

The manufacturers listed at the end of this book will supply ready-made card mounts in a large variety of sizes and colours.

*You will need:*
☐ Your finished embroidery
☐ A ready-made card mount
☐ Scissors
☐ Double-sided sticky tape
☐ Spraymount adhesive
☐ A large empty cardboard box
☐ A sheet of scrap paper

A ready-made mount will have three sections and a window already cut in it (Figs 35 and 36). Lay your embroidery on section (b) and trim the embroidery so that it is ½in (1.5cm) larger than the window. On the inside of the card, stick strips of double-sided sticky tape around the window and on section (a) as shown in Figs 35 and 36. The speckled area on section (a) indicates a squirt of an ozone-friendly aerosol adhesive such as Spraymount. This is sprayed on to give the embroidery a sticky surface to cling to; without it the embroidery has a tendency to ripple. Place the card with the inside facing you in an up-turned box. Cover sections (b) and (c) with a piece of scrap paper. Apply the Spraymount to section (a). The box and scrap paper will stop the adhesive going where it is not wanted.

Next, lay your embroidery face up on a flat surface. Remove the backing strips from the sticky

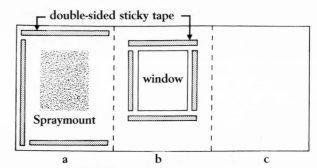

**Fig 35** *Mounting into a card with a rectangular or square window*

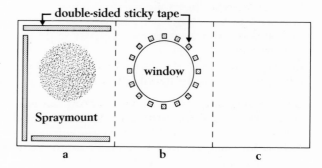

**Fig 36** *Mounting into a card with a circular or oval window*

tape on the card. With the outside of the card facing you, stick the window around your embroidery, making sure that it is straight. You might need several tries, but the embroidery peels off the sticky tape easily, so persevere until you are satisfied. Turn the card over and stick section (a) over section (b), smoothing the embroidery down onto the Spraymount. Write your greeting on section (c) and add any trimmings required.

## Method 2: Making your own card mounts

If your piece of embroidery will not fit into a ready-made mount, you will have to make your own mount. Choose card which is not too thin to stand up, nor so thick that it resembles board. Art shops stock sheets of suitable card in a variety of colours. If you are unable to find a colour subtle enough to complement your embroidery, buy white card and decorate it yourself. It is easy to apply a decorative paper to the surface of the card using Spraymount adhesive. Suitable papers include pastel and mottled writing paper (Designs 6, 21, 52 and 53), tissue paper (Design 75), mini-print wrapping paper or doll's house wallpaper (Designs 51, 77, 78, 79, 80).

For a more dramatic effect mottle the paper yourself (Design 76). To do this, take a sheet of paper and lay it on some newspaper. Pour some coloured ink into a saucer and dilute it with water to the strength required. Using a piece of old sponge, dab the ink onto the surface of the paper until it is covered. Experiment with different strengths of colour until you get the result you want, then allow the ink to dry. The paper will curl and buckle, but, when it is dry, a quick press with a warm iron on a flat surface will restore it to a state where it can be glued to card.

*You will need:*
☐ Your finished embroidery
☐ Card
☐ A pencil
☐ A metal ruler
☐ A scalpel-type craft knife
☐ A set-square
☐ Double-sided sticky tape
☐ Spraymount
☐ Graph paper with 10 squares to 1in (2.5cm) or a template from p118 traced onto thin card

Before you start, protect your working surface from cuts using thick cardboard. An artist's self-healing cutting mat provides a virtually indestructible surface and is a boon if you are going to do a lot of this work.

First cut the section of the card marked (b) and (c) in Fig 40. Mark cutting lines on the card with pencil and cut the card to the size required. Use the set-square to ensure that the sides are parallel, and cut the card using a metal ruler and a scalpel-type craft knife. Always stand up to cut, exerting a firm, downward pressure on the ruler and knife to avoid any slips. To achieve a professional-looking result, folds must be scored with a light cut that just pierces the top layer of the card. Score a line half way along the longest edge of the card, using the set-square (Fig 37). Fold the card in two.

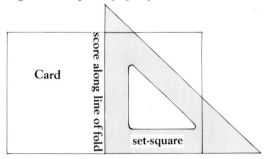

**Fig 37** *Using a set-square*

The pattern will tell you whether the card is to be side-folded (Fig 38a) or top-folded (Fig 38b).

Templates for square or rectangular windows are cut from graph paper. This cunningly ensures that the sides are parallel and the corners square without any effort on your part. Cut the graph paper to the size required, apply some Spraymount to the back and position the template on the card

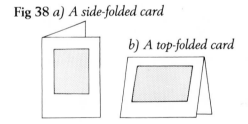

**Fig 38** *a) A side-folded card*

*b) A top-folded card*

(Fig 39), checking that the resulting window will frame your embroidery correctly. Ensure that all measurements marked (x) are equal. Cut around the template and remove it.

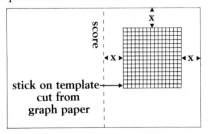

**Fig 39** *Putting the template on the card*

Templates for other shaped windows are given on p118. Trace the template onto thin card, cut out the template and, having applied the Spray-mount, cut out the window as above.

Circular windows need no template and are cut with a compass cutter, available from all good craft suppliers.

Next, cut the backing card marked section (a) in Fig 40 to the dimensions stated. To ensure that the card closes properly, trim off a ⅛in (1mm) strip along the edge which will lie next to the fold. Assemble your card (Fig 40) following the instructions for assembling a ready-made mount. If, in spite of all your careful measuring and cutting, your card stands at a drunken angle, do not despair and throw in the towel. Fold the card and remove the offending edges by cutting through all thicknesses. This should rectify the problem.

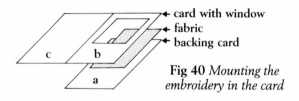

**Fig 40** *Mounting the embroidery in the card*

← card with window
← fabric
← backing card

c    b

a

## Method 3: Mounting padded embroidery onto the surface of a card

*You will need:*
☐ Your finished embroidery
☐ Card
☐ Thick card
☐ Wadding
☐ UHU glue

Cut your card to the size required, score it and fold it following the instructions for Method 2, but do not cut a window or a backing card. From thick card cut a base card to the size required. Cover this with a layer of wadding and wrap the embroidery

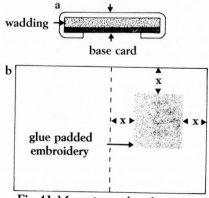

fabric

a

wadding

base card

b

x

◄ x ►    ◄ x ►

glue padded embroidery

**Fig 41** *Mounting embroidery using wadding*

around the wadding and base card. Glue the edges of the embroidery out of sight underneath the base card (Fig 41a). Now glue your padded embroidery to the surface of the card, ensuring that all measurements marked (x) are equal (Fig 41b).

## ALTERNATIVE WAYS TO USE DESIGNS
### Drawstring bag

Many of the designs in this book can be made up into drawstring bags if they are embroidered onto long strips of fabric. As each design is a different size it is impossible to give exact measurements to which to cut the fabric, except for Design 15. To assist you, the finished size of each piece of embroidery is given with the chart. Draw this measurement onto a strip of paper and use it as a paper pattern to help you to work out how much of the recommended fabric to cut. Check, by folding the paper pattern, that you are allowing sufficient fabric for folding and for turnings. When you are satisfied, cut the strip of fabric, then fold it in half and embroider the bottom of the design centrally above the fold.

When the embroidery is complete, fold the fabric in half along the long edge, right sides together, and make two side seams (Fig 42a). Leave a small opening at (c). Neaten all raw edges. Fold the fabric wrong sides together at (d). Seam around the bag at (e) and at (f) to make a channel for the drawstrings (Fig 42b). Turn the bag the right side out. Cut two lengths of ribbon. On the left-hand side of the bag, insert one ribbon into the channel and thread it all the way round the bag until it comes out of the hole it went into. Repeat with the other ribbon on the right-hand side of the bag.

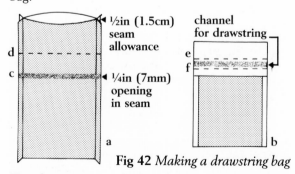

½in (1.5cm) seam allowance

channel for drawstring

d

c    ¼in (7mm) opening in seam

e
f

a    b

**Fig 42** *Making a drawstring bag*

### Tote bag

Many of the designs in this book can be made up into tote bags if they are embroidered onto long strips of fabric. As each design is a different size it is impossible to give exact measurements to which to cut the fabric, except for Designs 26, 29 and 44. To assist you, the finished size of each piece of embroidery is given with the chart. Draw this measurement onto a strip of paper and use it as a paper pattern to help you to work out how much of the recommended fabric to cut. Check, by folding the paper pattern, that you are allowing sufficient fabric for folding and for turnings. When you are satisfied, cut the strip of fabric, then fold it in half and embroider the bottom of the design centrally above the fold.

When the embroidery is complete, fold the fabric in half, right sides together, and make two side seams (Fig 43a). Neaten all raw edges. With wrong sides together, fold the top edge over and hemstitch in place all round the bag. Cut two lengths of grosgrain or other suitable ribbon. Fold the ribbon to form handles and slipstitch one handle on the front and another on the back of the bag (Fig 43b).

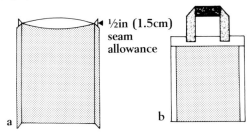

**Fig 43** *Making a tote bag*

### Purse

Some of the smaller designs in this book can be made up into purses if they are embroidered onto long strips of fabric. As each design is a different size it is impossible to give exact measurements to which to cut the fabric, except for Design 58. To assist you, the finished size of each piece of embroidery is given with the chart. Draw this measurement onto a strip of paper and use it as a paper pattern to help you to work out how much of the recommended fabric to cut. Check, by folding the paper pattern, that you are allowing sufficient fabric for folding and for turnings. When you are satisfied, cut the strip of fabric, then fold it as shown in Fig 44a and embroider the design centrally above the fold, on section (d).

When the embroidery is complete, neaten the two ends of the fabric by turning them to the wrong side and pressing them with a warm iron (Fig 44a). With right sides together fold section (d) over section (e) and make two side seams (Fig 44b). Turn the purse the right side out and, with a warm iron, press the two side pieces (g) into place (Fig 44c). Sew two loops of Russian braid to the top of the purse so that the loops protrude over the edge. Sew two decorative buttons to the front of the purse, to fit in the loops when the purse is folded. Make a similar but fractionally smaller purse from silky lining fabric. With wrong sides

together, insert the lining into the purse and slipstitch the two together to hide all turnings.

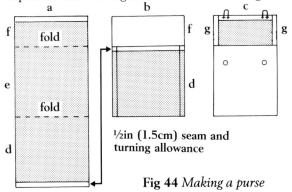

½in (1.5cm) seam and turning allowance

**Fig 44** *Making a purse*

### FINISHING TOUCHES

Suggestions for trimming cards are given with each chart but need not be followed to the letter unless you want your result to exactly match the sample in the photograph. You may have other trimmings that you wish to use and can substitute. If you are the 'squirrel' type, you will probably have collected oddments of braid, bits of ribbon, packets of sequins, beads and other goodies which can be of use. If not, explore your local haberdashery shop.

### Tassels

To make a tassel, cut two rectangular pieces of card the same size. The length of the tassel will be determined by the size of the card. Lay a loose length of thread between the two pieces of card; this will be used to attach the tassel to the embroidery. Wrap thread around the pieces of card (Fig 45a) until there is sufficient thread on the card to make a tassel of the thickness you require. Tie a knot in the loose length of thread to hold the tassel together. Slip your scissors between the two pieces of card and cut through the loops at (c). Tie a short length of thread firmly around the tassel at (d) (Fig 45b).

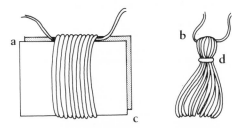

**Fig 45** *Making a tassel*

### Multi-looped bows

Wind a length of narrow ribbon in a figure-of-eight direction around a thumb and index finger (Fig

46). Repeat until you have the required number of loops. Tie another short length of ribbon firmly around point (x) to hold the loops in place. Trim the four ends to points and spread out the loops to form an attractive bow. Those of you who are very dextrous could manage this procedure unaided but it is easier to ask a friend, literally, to lend you a hand.

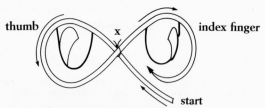

**Fig 46** *Making a multi-looped bow*

### Threading beads onto ribbon

If beads are threaded onto the ends of ribbons which have been knotted around cards, not only do they add extra decoration, but they also provide a weight which makes the ribbon hang well. To thread a bead with a small hole onto ribbon you will need to trim the ribbon to a long, fine point. Coat the point with glue and allow the glue to dry. You can now thread the rigid point through the bead. Push the bead up the ribbon (Fig 47a) and trim off the glued section (Fig 47b).

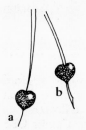

**Fig 47** *Threading beads onto ribbon*

### Envelopes

If you are unable to find an envelope to fit your finished card, it is a simple matter to make one. Choose paper or thin card in a colour which complements your work. Measure generously the card which is to go in the envelope and, with a pencil and ruler, draw this measurement onto your chosen paper. Draw the flaps of the envelope following the diagram (Fig 48). Draw the top and bottom flaps to measurement (a) plus ¼in (7mm) for the overlap. Draw the side flaps to measurement (b). Cut out the envelope and fold in the side flaps. Put a thin line of glue along the edge of the bottom flap and fold it over the side flaps. Insert your card and glue down the top flap.

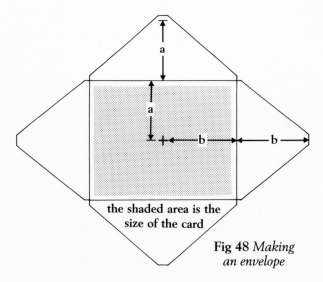

the shaded area is the size of the card

**Fig 48** *Making an envelope*

### Making a wallet

Cards with bulky trimmings, which will not fit into envelopes, can be presented in card wallets. Choose card for the wallet in a colour which complements your work. Measure your work generously and, with a pencil and ruler, draw this measurement onto the card you have chosen for the wallet. Draw the rest of the wallet following the diagram (Fig 49a), adjusting the measurements to fit your card. Cut, score and fold two side pieces, following the diagram (Fig 49a). Fold the wallet into its finished shape and glue the side pieces into position. Sew a decorative button or bead onto the flap and another onto the front of the wallet. Close the wallet by winding thread in a figure-of-eight around the buttons (Fig 49b).

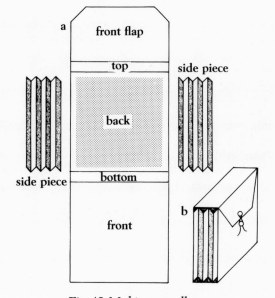

**Fig 49** *Making a wallet*

# Acknowledgements

I am indebted to Win Barry, Carol Burr, Ros Foster, Felicity Howatson, Margaret Jones, Elizabeth Lovesey, Sylvia Morgan, Penny Peberdy, Pam Rivers, Jean Sutton, Irene Vincent, and Joyce Watson for their invaluable help with stitching; many thanks to them all. Producing this book would have seemed an endless and lonely task without their help and constructive comments.

A special thank you goes to my fourteen-year-old daughter Nancy, who broke her leg and spent her summer holiday immobilised. Her loss was my gain, as she whiled away the time stitching more than twenty designs for me.

Many thanks also to Pam Griffiths, Brenda Morrison and Sarah Widdicombe at David & Charles for their enduring patience, encouragement and help; to Di Lewis for the care and attention to detail she gave to the photography; to Tony Foster of Warwick Studios, Emscote Road, Warwick who frames my work so expertly; and to David Cook, self-appointed slave-driver, unsurpassed forager and unpaid publicity agent.

I would like to thank especially all family and friends who supported me through the saga of 'the bad back'. Most of this book was designed, stitched, written and charted in a prone position, which I hope will offer some small encouragement to other sufferers not to throw in the towel (at least, not until they have embroidered it).

I am most grateful to the following suppliers for their generous assistance in the production of this book:

Offray Ribbon Ltd, Ashbury Road, Roscrea, Co Tipperary, Ireland (ribbon).

Berisfords Ltd, PO Box 2, Congleton, Cheshire CW12 1EF (ribbon).

Dunlicraft Ltd, Pullman Road, Wigston, Leicestershire LE8 2DY (Zweigart fabrics, DMC stranded cottons, card mounts – Design 36).

Coats Leisure Crafts Group Ltd, 39 Durham Street, Glasgow G41 1BS (Anchor stranded cottons).

Framecraft Miniatures Ltd, 148/150 High Street, Aston, Birmingham B6 4US (CraftaCards, porcelain bowls, lead crystal bowls, musical boxes, trays, key rings, brooches, Jar Lacys and other mounts). Framecraft products are also distributed by:

Anne Brinkley Designs Inc, 21 Ransom Road, Newton Centre, Mass. 02159 USA.

Ireland Needlecraft, 16 Mavron Street, Ashwood 3147 Australia.

The Campden Needlecraft Centre, High Street, Chipping Campden, Glos (needlecraft supplies, baby's bibs, card mounts – Designs 32, 33, 34, 35, 41, 48, 49 (gold), 72).

Artisan, 22 High Street, Pinner, Middlesex HA5 5PW (needlecraft supplies).

The Voirrey Embroidery Centre, Brimstage Hall, Brimstage, Wirrall L63 6JA (needlecraft supplies, key ring – Design 38).

David Springett, 21 Hillmorton Road, Rugby, Warks CV22 5DF (miniature lace bobbins).

The Sewing Basket, 4 Chapel Alley, Formby, Liverpool L37 4DL (card mounts – Designs 46, 47, 55, 69).

Letraset UK Ltd, 195/203 Waterloo Road, London SE1 8XJ (Letrafilm).

My thanks also to the following for their assistance with other supplies:

Janet Coles Beads, Perdiswell Cottage, Bilford Road, Worcester WR8 8QA (beads; flower, leaf and heart beads, sequins and artificial flowers).

Spangles, 1 Casburn Lane, Burwell, Cambs CB5 0ED (beads and some of the trimmings for Design 48).

Craft Creations Ltd, 2–4 Harpers Yard, Ruskin Road, Tottenham, London N17 8NE (card mounts – Designs 1b, 59, 68).

Impress, Slough Farm, Westhall, Halesworth, Suffolk IP19 8RN (card mounts, gift tag mounts).

Paperchase, 213 Tottenham Court Road, London W1P 9AF (card, decorative paper and doll's house wallpaper).

Rod Waspe, Millar Court, Kenilworth, Warks (stationery).

# Index

Advent calendar, *see* Christmas
All Fools' Day, 30–1
Alphabet and Numerals, 114–17;
    nursery, 82–3
Autumn birthday, 56
Autumn sunset, 112

Babies, 76–86; alphabet, 82–3;
    Christening, 84–6; shower, 78;
    twins, 79
Beatrice, Princess, birthday
    memento, 4
Birthdays, 52–7; special, 58–63
Bridal shower, 67
Brooches, 29

Chanukkah, 94
Chinese New Year, 96
Christening, 84–6
Christmas, 8–23; Advent calendar,
    14–19; Goodwill to all men, 13;
    Nativity scene, 10–11; Peace on
    earth, 12; Twelve Days of
    Christmas, 20–3
Church wedding, 70
Confirmation, 89

Diwali, 98
Drawstring Bag, 124
Driving test, 103

Early Year, The, 24–31; All Fools'
    Day, 30–1; Hogmanay, 28; New
    Year, 26–7; Patron Saints' Day
    brooches, 29; St Patrick's Day, 28
Easter, 36–9; Easter bonnet
    pincushion, 37; Easter eggs, 39;
    Easter gift tag, 38; He is risen, 37
Eighteenth birthday, 61
Engagement, 66–7
Envelopes, 126

Father's Day, 40, 43
Festivals, calendar of, 6–7;
    Chanukkah, 94; Chinese New
    Year, 96; Diwali, 98; Id Ul-Fitr,
    96–7; Mardi Gras, 99; Rosh
    Hashanah, 95; worldwide, 92–9
First birthday, 60
First Communion, 89
Fortieth birthday, 62
Fourth of July, 44–7; bald eagle, 47;
    jelly bean bag, 46; Uncle Sam, 45
Friendship, 106–7
Fruits of the Earth, 51

Garden (miniature), 108
Get Well Soon, 104
Golden Wedding, 74–5
Good Luck, 102
Graduation, 103

Hallowe'en, 48–9
Harvest and Thanksgiving, 50–1
Hogmanay, 28

Id Ul-Fitr, 96
Instructions, general, 5

Lord is my Shepherd, The, 91

Mardi Gras, 99
Marriage, 64–75; anniversaries,
    72–5; bridal shower, 67;
    engagement, 66; ring pillow, 68–9
Medicine tray, 104
Mother's Day, 40–2

New home, 105
New Year, 26–7
Numerals, 115–17
Nursery alphabet, 82–3

Patron Saint's Day, 29
Pincushions, 37, 105; pin pillow, 34
Pot-pourri heart sachet, 41
Purse, 125

Registry Office wedding, 71
Religious occasions, 87–91;
    bookmark, 88, 90; Confirmation,
    89; First Communion, 89
Rice sack, 67

Ring pillow, 68–9
Rosh Hashanah, 95
Ruby Wedding, 72

Seventieth birthday, 63
Silver wedding, 75
Sixteenth birthday, 61
Sixtieth birthday, 62–3
Special birthdays, 58–63
Spring, 110
Spring birthday, 54
Stitching, 120–2
St Patrick's Day, 28
Summer, 111
Summer birthday, 55

Techniques, 119–26; beads, etc,
    122; designing, 119; fabric,
    119–21; finishing, 125–6;
    mounting, 122–4; paint, 119
Templates, 117–8
Thank You, 102
Thanksgiving, 50–1
Thread, general, 5
Tote Bag, 124
Trick-or-Treat Bag, 49
Twenty-first birthday, 61

Valentines, 32–5; Cupid's arrow,
    35; Roses are red, 33; Victorian
    pin pillow, 34

Weddings, *see* Marriage;
    anniversaries, 72–5
Wicked Witch, 49
Winter birthday, 57
Winter snow scene, 113

---

### PUZZLE SOLUTION (p30)

ECIVDA spells out ADVICE backwards and this
is the clue to reading the message. Instead of
starting to read at the top left-hand corner, try the
bottom right-hand corner. By reading from the
bottom then the top in sequence you will discover
the following:

*When man to man is so unjust*
*In deed or word you should not trust*
*Take my advice never ask to borrow*
*But pay today and trust tomorrow.*
*Author unknown*